MW01172250

Forgiveness
From the Heart

Healing for a Wounded World

Dr. Wayne C. Solomon
Dr. Philip M. Bonaparte Sr.

Contact Information
Wayne C. Solomon
(321) 759-9777
forgivenessfromtheheart@yahoo.com
Philip M. Bonaparte
(609)-658-8702

Dedication

To my friend and brother,
Pastor Hugh A. Bair, PhD.
a man with a truly forgiving heart.
Wayne C. Solomon, D Min.

To my wife, Tracey S. Bonaparte,
who has stood with me over the years and
whose acts of forgiveness are exemplary.
Philip M. Bonaparte, M.D.

Acknowledgements

There are numerous people who have been instrumental in making this volume available. They include the members of New Hope Church of God and the New Hope and Florida Church of God Prayer-lines' participants. We are especially grateful to those who graciously allowed us to share their experiences to the benefit of the Kingdom of God. Only heaven will reveal the impact that your stories would have had on millions of lives. We also wish to acknowledge, Karen Clark for her transcribing of the audio taping of our live sessions. Thanks to Monica Solomon for her invaluable work in layout, formatting and editing, and Philip Bonaparte II, for his assistance with this project.

Table of Contents

Forgiveness Prayer

"Lord I praise Your Holy Name and thank You for Your mercies. I come before Your presence with singing. I rejoice and thank You for the privilege that I have to approach Your throne in the Name of Your Son, Jesus Christ. I ask for Your forgiveness and acknowledge Jesus as my Pasqual Lamb upon the brazen altar. Thank You for Calvary's cross. Jesus, You said, 'As Moses lifted up the serpent in the wilderness, so the Son of man will be lifted up.' I remember Your agony, Your sacrifice, Your humility, Your shame, so I can have access to the presence of the Almighty. I come boldly on the merits of the blood and in the Name of Your Son Jesus Christ. Dear Father, I thank You for allowing Your Son Jesus to die so I can live. What love! Greater love has no man than this that a man lay down his life for his friend. For You, God, so loved this world that You sent Your only begotten Son, Jesus. What love! that You laid down Your life for me. I am eternally grateful and so humbly ask You to forgive me because I have not expressed my gratitude as much as I should. Remind me that it is about Your sacrifice, not the cross, but You, Jesus. It is not about the tomb but it is about You, the person, the very personification of forgiveness. So I yield myself to you today to be a forgiving person in Your sacred name. Amen!"

4

FOREWORD

By R. Lamar Vest
Former General Overseer of Church of God
President Emeritus of American Bible Society

What is the most difficult thing for you to believe about the Christian faith? For many it's forgiveness. Why? Because forgiveness is one of the most difficult things for humans to do. It isn't easy to forgive, especially when someone has betrayed you, damaged your reputation or committed an egregious offense against a member of your family. However, those who have chosen to follow Jesus Christ realize that forgiveness is a central theme of His message. The essence of the Christian life is forgiveness, and it's a two-way street. We are to forgive as we have been forgiven.

So we know that we are to forgive, but the paramount question is "how?" Drs. Wayne Solomon, DMin and Philip Bonaparte, M.D. in their book *"Forgiveness from the Heart"* deal with that question in a profound and yet practical manner. It is, without question, one of the best works I have read regarding this incredibly significant subject.

From their professional backgrounds, the authors examine the subject through the lenses of medical, psychological and theological knowledge. Most importantly, however, they approach the subject as two men who have faced the challenge of forgiving and being forgiven up close and personal, and they share their experiences in a most insightful manner. A fundamental principle that permeates this book is that the most amazing thing about Christianity is forgiveness. God's forgiveness of us demands that we forgive others, because grace brings such responsibility and obligation. A forgiving spirit shows that we are true followers of Jesus Christ. To ever lose the miracle of forgiveness would be the death of the Christian faith.

The byproduct of un-forgiveness is guilt and bitterness, which psychologists recognize as a central fact in personality disorders. The biblical answer to both is forgiveness. Human forgiveness can never free the person being forgiven of any sin they may have committed. Only Jesus can do that. Human forgiveness simply means we are freeing others from our personal judgment. Forgiveness may or may not be accepted by the offender, but it is extraordinarily freeing to the person doing the forgiving.

I commend the authors for their very thorough exegesis of forgiveness texts in Scripture. Also, I commend them for their emphasis on the importance of prayer in practicing *"Forgiveness from the Heart."* The beautifully and expressive prayers they share at the end of each chapter are worth the purchase of the book. It is only through prayer that we are able to express, from the heart, the quality of forgiveness with which we have been forgiven by God. The authors explain the three-step process of forgiveness with the acronym ACT: Admission, Confession, and Transformation. With each step we take toward forgiveness, we move toward spiritual wholeness. Forgiveness, as illuminated by Drs. Solomon and Bonaparte will, indeed, bring peace to us individually and to our world.

Those of us who have experienced God's forgiveness as Paul described in Col. 2:14 can never be un-forgiving toward our fellow humans. What grace we have been shown! Now, we are obligated to share that forgiving grace with others. **"Christ has utterly wiped out the damning evidence of broken laws and commandments which always hung over our heads, and has completely annulled it by nailing it over his own head on the cross."** -Col 2:14. It is time for the Body of Christ to practice "Forgiveness From the **Heart.**"

Introduction

If you live long enough you will end up offending someone, (*Luke 17:1*, "It is impossible that no offenses should come…" NKJV). We offend others either intentionally or inadvertently. The opposite is also true, we are offended by others and at times the offense seems to last a lifetime. Though we seek forgiveness for the wrongs we have done, it is often difficult for us to forgive those who have harmed, used or abused us. When someone asks you to forgive them, what is your response to their apology? Do you say, "you are forgiven?" Do your actions support genuine forgiveness? In our society, we find it easier to focus on the negative, the mistakes and failures of the past and not on the hopes and the beauty of the now and the future.

In this book, Forgiveness From the Heart, you will find what the bible teaches us about forgiveness. It explains the expectation of your Father in forgiving those who have wronged or hurt you. It looks at the obstacles that prevent you from forgiving and gives you practical steps to be taken in creating a culture of forgiveness. How do you make forgiveness an ACT? How could you use forgiveness as a lethal weapon and why do you need a heart transplant? You will find real life experiences of several Christians who are transparent in revealing how they overcame forgiving those who appeared unforgiveable. It is our prayer that you will apply these tried and proven principles recorded in this book to your life and receive freedom from your past as together we create a culture of forgiveness.

Dr. Philip M. Bonaparte M.D.

Chapter 1

❦

Acting like your Father

When we accept God's pardon, we are able to have a forgiving spirit and be more like Jesus.

Mark 11:25
And when ye stand praying, forgive, if ye have ought against any: that your Father also which is in heaven may forgive you your trespasses.

Economy airline flights are often non-stop and affordable. Their destination airports are usually smaller, security lines are shorter, parking lots are closer to the terminals, and there are no frills on these flights; no free food, no free extra drinks, no movies and the seats may recline. I appreciate the small bag of snacks and a drink or some water that is given during the flight. When the plane landed in

Trenton, Philip was waiting to pick me up. He rolled up in a black SUV and after he placed my bag in the trunk and we greeted each other, we prayed in thanksgiving for my safe arrival and for the three days of consecration I had flown to New Jersey to be a part of.

"God gave me a word this morning as I led the prayer-line" he said. "What is it?" I enquired. "Forgiveness" he responded. Philip and I have been friends for over 30 years. He is not a shallow Christian. His deep love for God has been an inspiration to me. Dr. Selwyn Arnold spent the last years of his life mentoring us both. We miss Brother Arnold. Like me, Philip has had his share of lumps from this life and I suspect he too has a list of people to inform that he forgave them. We stopped at the Barber Shop and got haircuts then we arrived at the Church.

New Hope is one Church in three locations of New Jersey: East Windsor, Long Branch and Trenton. Dr. Philip Bonaparte (MD) has led the Church for over a decade. New Hope Church started in his home with his wife and two kids and has grown to several hundreds of members and adherents. This church was featured in the July 2013 issue of Charisma News as one of The fastest growing Churches in America that you have not heard of. We pulled into the parking lot at the East Windsor church and entered the sanctuary. My bags were placed near the front pew almost in the altar area. I was not really concerned about accommodations for the three days ahead, I was eager to hear more from Philip.

"I wrote a booklet in 1986 titled Forgiveness from the Heart" I said to Philip. "Do you have a copy?" He questioned. "No but I know who has one" I said. "Who does?" Philip asked. "Well it is an 87-year-old brother in Trinidad and he has no intention of giving it up, even his son could not get it from him. I have a picture of the cover that his son took" I quipped. Following a healthy laugh our conversation got going and I realized that it centered around some of the same thoughts of the 1986 booklet. "The Holy Spirit directed me during the Prayer-line devotion this morning and revealed several scriptures to me" Philip continued. My attention became laser focused and I was ready to drink in every word the Lord had spoken. Soon I understood why God had arranged for me to come to New Jersey.

This time of consecration became the catalyst for a journey into the domain of <u>Forgiveness From the Heart</u>, for thousands of people around the world as well as for Philip and me. We took out our Bibles and began digging for the priceless forgiveness treasure chest God had deposited in His Holy Word for His children.

It began with Matthew 6:6 Jesus said "But thou, when thou prayest, enter into thy closet, and when thou hast shut thy door, pray to thy Father which is in secret; and thy Father which seeth in secret shall reward thee openly." This is the right way to conduct a powerful and successful prayer life. Public praying has its place but secret prayer is encouraged in this text.

In that time of petition, Jesus raised a salient factor for a prayer that God accepts in verse Matthew 6:12,

"And forgive us our debts, as
we forgive our debtors."

Forgiveness is the willing excusing or pardoning of one who offends you. Many Christians struggle with forgiveness. Both men and women have this challenge and long for a way to take the right steps to ending a lifestyle of un-forgiveness. Maybe those of us who love much get hurt the most. However, regardless of how hurt we have been, God wants us to forgive and let it go, because He knows it is best for us. It is not that He is standing over our heads with a big stick saying "you better forgive or I will crack your skull." He wants us to forgive because it will restore us to spiritual, emotional and physical health.

In Matthew 6:14-15 Jesus said "For if ye forgive men their trespasses, your heavenly Father will also forgive you: But if ye forgive not men their trespasses, neither will your Father forgive your trespasses." Some of us have asked God to forgive us but still carry the heavy weight of the sin of un-forgiveness by not letting go and forgiving someone who has hurt us. I guess the difficulty is to determine a path for moving from un-forgiveness to forgiveness. If we take a closer look at one of the parables Jesus gave, we may get some traction in the direction of a lifestyle of forgiveness.

Jesus used many parables to illustrate the epic truths He wished to convey. Parables are earthly stories with heavenly meanings. One such story is found in Matthew chapter 18:23-35. He begins this quintessential discourse by analogizing the Kingdom of Heaven to a king who attempted to collect outstanding loans from his debtors. One such debtor owed him ten thousand talents or 1.2 billion US dollars. The debtor could not pay so the king ordered that the man, his wife and children be sold into slavery and his possessions be sold also to cover the debt. The man fell at the king's feet and begged for a chance to pay it all back. The king was very compassionate in this story and he allowed the man to go free and erased the entire debt. The same forgiven man saw one of his fellow servants who owed him one hundred denarii or 2,000 US dollars.

The forgiven man seized the one who owed him and demanded his money be paid immediately. The debtor was not able to pay and begged for mercy and for a chance to pay it all back. But he would not be merciful. Instead, he had him arrested and put in jail, until the whole debt was paid. When others saw what had happened they were displeased and reported the injustice to the king.

The king called the man and said, (*Are you serious?*)[1] 'You evil servant! I forgave your entire

---

[1] Authors' insertion

debt when you begged me for mercy. Shouldn't you be compelled to be merciful to your fellow servant who asked for mercy?' The king was infuriated and arrested the man requiring him to pay back the entire debt. Jesus said "And that's exactly what my Father in heaven is going to do to each one who doesn't forgive unconditionally anyone who asks for mercy." (Matthew 18:35 Message Version)

You may ask "what does that have to do with me?" Simply this, you and I can never pay the Lord God in heaven for what Jesus did in taking care of our debt. There is no monetary or non-monetary compensation capable of making things right between God and us, it is priceless, yet when you and I mess up, even as Christians and we go to the Father in heaven, He forgives us of our sins. In the same way that we are forgiven God expects us to forgive those who offend us.

The quality of forgiveness is the same as that of God's quality of forgiveness. Of course, we owe God so much that repayment is impossible. All He asks is that we be merciful and forgive our brothers and sisters just as He has forgiven us. Forgiving is not always easy to do. Trying to let things go is a task, so we need to rely on God to help us because this is what He expects of us and we want to please Him. In spite of our imperfections we are trying to get to heaven and do not want un-forgiveness to be a hindrance.

If someone owes you money and did not repay as scheduled, and has asked you for mercy to extend the repayment time, or even to forgive the loan and you can forego the loan, especially if this entire matter is causing you grief, maybe you can call them and say, "I know that you are having difficulty with repaying the loan I gave you. I am willing to work with you and give you more time so we can resolve this matter in an amicable way and hope that we can move forward with our relationship."

Here is a case of a sister who called in on the New Hope Prayer-line to comment on this topic. "Praise God. I really, really want to give thanks and praise to God this morning. I got up before five o'clock. I was so uneasy and I just couldn't sleep. I know what you said about forgiveness. I've called in on the prayer line lots of times for prayer for my friend to pay me back. She owes me over forty-seven thousand dollars. You said 'write it down.' I already wrote it down; I already sent a text that I can forward to you. Before you said send a text, I sent a text to two people and said 'I forgive you because I want to make it to heaven.' Almost a hundred thousand dollars is owed to me. I said 'God I know You are going to provide for me, so I'm going to let it go because it's been on my heart.' I don't have a job, the kids are in day care, but I said, 'God I know you are a Sustainer.' This has been on my heart and this teaching is doing so much for me, I just want to thank God for you for bringing it forth and for birthing that in me to say 'I forgive and I let it go.' Now that I did it I feel so much lighter, I feel so much better. Also, I didn't feel well, I couldn't even speak yesterday. However, I didn't even have to ask for prayer this morning on the prayer line. As you were going along teaching on forgiveness, I was claiming my healing. I just asked God for healing and now I can speak. Praise the Lord."

Sometimes you just need to let it go! God is your source! The God you serve is the magnanimous God of the universe. Believe that same God can give you every dollar owed to you. Forgive the person, don't hold any malice in your heart, do not allow yourself to be dragged down into the gutter of un-forgiveness. Forgive! Do not be surprised that after you tell some people, who are true born again believers that you forgave them they will repay you. Those that refuse to pay are to be left in God's hands.

Let's take a look at Luke chapter 17; Jesus said to the disciples "It is impossible that no offenses should come, but woe to him through whom they do come." In the world we live offenses are a given, we are offended and we offend. We can never live a life without offending someone or someone offending us. So do not be surprised when it happens, even between brothers and sisters in the home and even in the church.

We are brothers and sisters in Christ but we will offend one another from time to time. You know there is no perfect church and if there was one the moment you show up it will become imperfect. Sometimes we offend intentionally and at other times unintentionally. Offense will come Jesus said. Offenses are things that can cause people to stumble. Offenses happen. But the Lord said "but woe unto him by whom they come." Woe means "cursed is the one …. that makes it happen."

Jesus said it would have been better for that person to take "a millstone" a huge grinding stone that is extremely heavy, "and tie it around his neck, and throw himself into the sea, than to cause offense to one of his children and so cause him or her to stumble." What does it mean? We in the body of Christ should be extremely careful how we talk to one another and how we treat one another. There are a lot of people who left the church, some of whom may wind up in hell because of our irresponsible, unforgiving and offending behaviors. Stop saying to yourself "I am so upset, I am so mad, I will not forgive, and I will hold it to my grave. I will curse you because you have cursed me." That is not of God. Be careful because you can cause somebody to not make it to heaven or cause some believer that is serving God to backslide, as they are not able to handle what you have done to them.

Jesus follows up with these words in Luke 17: 3-5 "Take heed to yourselves" or watch out, pay attention, exercise caution for "If your brother sins against you, **rebuke him**; and if he repents, **forgive him**. And if he sins against you seven times in a day, and seven times in a day returns to you, saying, 'I repent,' you shall **forgive him**. And the apostles said to the Lord, Increase our faith." Verse number 3 says: If your brother or sister sins against you,

you have the right and spiritual responsibility to rebuke him or her. A rebuke is not to be seen as a bad thing. Let them know what they did to you was wrong. Now be careful to do so in a loving and considerate manner, lest the situation is made worse. Galatians 6:1 speaks about restoration of an offending person, in a spirit of meekness.

Even though you have been offended it does not give you the right to retaliate in the same manner in which the offense was made. If the offender cursed you, do not curse back. If they struck you, do not strike back. Your spiritual duty is to rebuke, not punish. Let the offender know what they did was wrong according to the Word of God. It will also be helpful to show from scripture what God expects.

Now going a little further, Jesus said "if they repent, forgive them." You may ask "why?" This will release you from the weight and pain that holding a grudge inflicts. The offender also benefits when they acknowledge they did wrong, it helps them to have the proper disposition for forgiveness and restoration. In addition, Jesus expects that the person, who has wronged you, should ask for forgiveness, if they are a part of the body of Christ.

If they do it, Jesus said to say to them, "I forgive you."

The next verse gives us a scenario of a greater magnitude. If that same person, who wronged you, sinned against you, upset you seven times! Did He say in a lifetime? Did he say seven times in thirty years? Did he say seven times in a year, a month, a week? No, He said, "in a day!" That is a tall order! In anger, some may respond by saying, "OH NO! three strikes and you are out! You did it to me three times, you are not going to make a fool out of me! Once was too much!" If we speak like that, just remember that's how the world talks. The believer has a different language and culture, the language and culture of the Kingdom of God, so we must strive to speak like children of the King.

Ours is a language of love and forgiveness. Anger and revenge are not traits of our lifestyle. Our behaviors are motivated by love, mercy, caring, compassion, building each other up, strengthening the weak, bearing the burdens of others and forgiveness. This does not promise to be an easy task but it is the way of God, He forgives us and expects us to speak and act like Him since we are His children.

If anyone told me that they heard my daughters swearing or being disrespectful to anyone I would be surprised, and would refuse to believe that person, because my wife and I trained our children to act responsibly and respectfully. In fact, they behave better when they are not with me. When they were little, I spent time playing with them. I invested countless hours praying over them while they were in the womb and after they were born. Almost every morning, winter, spring, summer or fall, I took my older daughter to a park and spent time with her praying for her, teaching her to appreciate nature and just allowing what's in me and on me to rub off on her.

I never use vile language and I do not even put up with television programming that is laced with profanity. So, there is a culture of pure speech in our home and our daughters have developed around the purity my wife and I demand of them therefore, I know how they speak. In the same way, God knows how we should speak and if we are truly His children we will speak like Him, love like Him and forgive like He does.

Some may say "well Pastor that's easy for you, you are a man of God" or even "you are a man, it is easier for men than women to move on and forgive." Gender is not a factor in this matter, both men and women have trouble forgiving. There are some men who just do not want to or feel they cannot let things go and forgive. This is not a woman problem! This is a human problem. He expects women and men to forgive. I want to challenge you, if you are struggling with un-forgiveness, take your first step and pray this prayer of forgiveness:

"Dear Lord I come to You in Jesus name, I acknowledge that You are a merciful and compassionate God, Who forgives the vilest of men and women. You forgave me and accepted me in spite of my sinful condition. You did not forgive me conditionally but in unconditional love. You opened the door of Your heart and let me in. So Lord, help me to open the door of my heart and let my brother, my sister in. Help me to walk the untrodden path to my brother, my sister and extend the olive branch of forgiveness to them. I remind myself that I am not worthy of Your forgiveness so, I fall at Your feet and ask You to have mercy on me as I have mercy on my brother, my sister. I am sorry for harboring feelings of vengeance, please cleanse me from them. I repent for holding onto my hurt and pain, so I could remain in the doldrums of un-forgiveness. Lord I repent and I submit to Your holy will as I continue to pray 'forgive me my transgressions as I

forgive those who transgress against me.' Thank You Lord, in Jesus name. Amen!"

Chapter 1 Review

1. Summarize Matthew 6: 12-15 in one sentence.
2. Summarize Matthew 6:12-15 in one word.
3. What can be said about the nature of ancient kings in Matthew 18?
4. Is it practical to forgive someone seven times in one day? If so what will you need to do emotionally, spiritually, physically and mentally each time you are asked to forgive?
5. When we forgive we show that we are God's children. Explain.
6. Do women have more difficulty with forgiving than men? If so why? If not why not?

Chapter 2

⬥

Seven Times

God will give you the spiritual strength and grace to forgive, as you have been forgiven by Him.

Luke 17:4
"And if he trespass against thee seven times in a day, and seven times in a day turn again to thee, saying, I repent; thou shalt forgive him."

"Machine gunfire, exploding howitzer shells, the crack of automatic rifle bullets, cannon fire, rocket launcher projectiles, field artillery rounds fired from anti-aircraft guns ripping through the air, armored vehicles roaring outside, patrol boats tearing through the calm Caribbean Sea and low flying fighter aircraft zooming over the tops of coconut trees. US Marines, 5,000 strong by sea, air and land, amid shouts, screams and shrieks that pierce the humid tropical air, brought mind shattering fear to the hearts of the over 800 young medical students, enrolled at the St. George's School of Medicine, the Americans had come to rescue.

Operation Urgent Fury had begun. Huddled in the classrooms and labs of the School, we hid until the Marines took complete control of the campus. By war's end, 59 Cubans were killed, 25 wounded, 45 Grenadians died, 337 wounded, 19 Americans dead, 119 wounded and all the Medical Students unharmed.

I cannot adequately describe the fear and anxiety that became part and parcel of the lives of the peace-loving people of Grenada. Suspicion and terror descended on this little paradise island when nine cabinet ministers and the Prime Minister were assassinated in October 1983. Soon brother was turned against brother with assault rifles in hands. Lies and deception were the order of the day. Cuban forces occupied this Isle of Spice. Churches were ordered to shut their doors. A shoot-on-sight curfew was in force.

I was listed on the Regime's most wanted list because I preached every Friday in the public market square against communism and the atheistic aspects of socialism. In early summer of 1983, a reporter did an article on the medical school. I was featured in that report as a Grenadian success story. He asked me about what I thought about the situation in Grenada, stating that it was off the record.

The Reporter had turned off his recorder, and stopped writing. He told me I was free to speak but not to talk about the government, so I spoke freely. The next thing I knew, he quoted me in a syndicated report that was published throughout the Caribbean. My sister, Veronica, sent me a clipping of the article from a St. Thomas newspaper. I believe it was also featured in news reports in Barbados and Trinidad and Tobago. The Grenadian authorities started looking for me, but God hid me among the students on the campus of the Medical School. My name was on a list of people targeted for assassination. That list was discovered after the US Marines rescued us and took control of the island. The betrayals, the deceptions, the murders, the abuse and intimidation had torn the country apart.

In the aftermath of the horror in that tiny paradise, restoration of the nation was only possible because the word of Jesus was obeyed. People forgave!"[2]

"And if he trespass against thee seven times in a day, and seven times in a day turn again to thee, saying, I repent; thou shalt forgive him." (Luke 17:4)

There is something fascinatingly distinct about the number seven:

- Sunday, Monday, Tuesday, Wednesday, Thursday, Friday, Saturday—The Seven Days of the Week.
- Jupiter, Mars, Mercury, The Moon, Venus, Saturn, The Sun—The Seven Classical Planets.
- Red, Orange, Yellow, Green, Blue, Indigo Violet—The Seven Colors of the Rainbow.
- The Arctic Ocean, the Indian Ocean, the North Atlantic Ocean, the South Atlantic Ocean, the North Pacific Ocean, the South

---

[2] *Dr. Philip Bonaparte's personal experience*

Pacific Ocean, the Southern Ocean—The Seven Seas.

- Africa, Antarctica, Asia, Australia, Europe, North America, and South America—The Seven Continents.
- A, B, C, D, E, F, G—The Seven musical notes.
- The Colossus of Rhodes, The Great Pyramid of Giza, The Hanging Gardens of Babylon, The Lighthouse of Alexandria, The Mausoleum at Halicarnassus, The Statue of Zeus at Olympia, The Temple of Artemis at Ephesus—The Seven Wonders of the Ancient World.

After the number one, the number seven occurs most in the Bible (735 times).

God instructed the Hebrews to observe Seven Sacred Feasts namely: Passover, Unleavened Bread, First-fruits, Pentecost, Day of Atonement, the Feast of Trumpets and the Feast of Tabernacles (Leviticus 23). Leviticus 16, records that on the Day of Atonement the High Priest sprinkled the sacrificial blood upon the Mercy seat seven times.

According to Joshua chapter 6, Israel marched around Jericho seven times on the seventh day.

2 Kings 5:14 records that "Naaman the leper went down and dipped himself seven times in the Jordan, according to the saying of the man of God: and his flesh came again like unto the flesh of a little child, and he was clean."

Jesus gave seven sayings while on the Cross. In the Book of Revelation, we see seven churches, seven golden candlesticks, seven Spirits, seven stars, seven seals, seven trumpets, seven bowls of God's wrath, seven persons, seven judgements and seven new things. The number seven is the most sacred number to the Jewish people; it expresses Completeness and Spiritual Perfection.

The number seven seems to have distinct significance in the natural world and in the spiritual world.

So, in Luke 17:4 when Jesus said "forgive seven times in a day" He was saying, to forgive totally until you are complete. Forgiving others completes you and is God's way of perfecting you spiritually through each episode of forgiveness.

Jesus does not use this number arbitrarily. It is sometimes called God's number because of its unique uses throughout scripture, history and even in nature itself. Seven clearly speaks of completeness. So when seven is included like in 17, 27, 37, 47, 57, 67, 70, 77, 87, 97, 107, 2017 etc., it is symbolic in the spiritual realm. There are blessings and promises from God that can be claimed surrounding the number seven or its derivatives. Seven is a perfect number, it is a complete number. God made the earth in six days and rested on the seventh.

Seven is God's number and it is salient to forgiveness. Jesus used the perfect number, seven, meaning that for whatever number of times you are offended, it is your responsibility to forgive. You may say, 'Pastor, it is not fair.' And I will have to respond, 'it has nothing to do with being fair. It is about whether or not you want to please God.

For some people, it may even be of greater consequence. It may be about whether they want to go to heaven. It is a choice we all have to make. I am aware that I am coming across really hard, really, really, really hard but I want everyone to grasp it. If you are unable to find it within you to forgive that person, who may have offended you, you may well be continuing in un-forgiveness from which you need to be delivered. The pain is real and therefore with God's help, good Christian counsel and in time, deliverance will come. It is my prayer that after reading this book you will be on the road to deliverance and healing[3].

Being willing to forgive may determine your eternal destiny, so God wants you to start working on it now if you are still struggling with the sin of un-forgiveness. Remember in Matthew 18:35 Jesus made a contingency statement when He said 'Your heavenly Father will not forgive you if you do not forgive one who offends you.' You need to forgive those who trespass against you or who are debtors to you. You need to forgive them because your heavenly Father has forgiven you.

This is the Word of God and I have not even scratched the surface as there are so many scriptures that speak to this God-given mandate. For instance, Ephesians chapter 4 verse 32, says 'And be ye kind one to another, tenderhearted, forgiving one another, even as God for Christ's sake hath forgiven you. To be kind and tenderhearted means to show compassion.

---

[3] Psalm 27 is an excellent message of comfort. Read it prayerfully.

Some people are able to show compassion to suffering people they have never seen, in some other part of the world, but find it hard to be tenderhearted and compassionate to those who they interact with regularly. God expects us to show compassion to those close to us that may have offended us as well. Tenderheartedness begins with forgiving one another!

In Luke 17, Jesus said it is impossible for us not to offend one another. We will offend one another; it is the world we live in. In marriages, I guarantee you, you or your spouse will do something that my cause you to offend each other. Your children may offend you or you will offend them. Friends offend each other, your boss may offend you and your workmates may offend you or you may offend them. You may be offended in school. It happens between grown up brothers and sisters who have their own families. It may happen in church.

Our grand-parents in the Caribbean used to say, 'tongue and teeth live in the same mouth, yet they clash'. Once you are alive you will offend and be offended. Jesus said expect offenses. Someone will rub you the wrong way and you may ask "what should I do?" God says forgive them! Forgiving one another is God's way. Man's way is taking revenge.

Our example is Jesus Christ. Just as our Father in heaven through Christ has forgiven us, so ought we to forgive others. For those of us who have not forgiven your offenders, I want you to take some time, may be about a half an hour or so and just recap what we have been discussing. Then prepare to act: ask God to forgive you for the spirit of un-forgiveness, ask God to deliver you from the spirit of un-forgiveness. Finally, as the Holy Spirit brings your offenders to your remembrance, make a list of the names. Call them up, send a text message, send them email, or contact them on Facebook. You are sure that these people wronged you. You were in the right as far as you know. When you make contact, you do not need to go into details. Be brief, be sincere and be clear. Let them know that "God has been dealing with me about our situation; I would like us to work towards a reconciliation. I forgive you and look forward to having a good relationship." Then let it go! Tell God that you let it go! Tell people you have let it go. Testify without calling names saying that you let it go. It will help you to be delivered and healed.

To get the most out of fasting, forgiveness is critical. Un-forgiveness can hinder your fast. Fasting is to be done with a forgiving heart and with the right motives.

Isaiah 58 explains the fast that pleases God.

"6 Is not this the fast that I have chosen? to loose the bands of wickedness, to undo the heavy burdens, and to let the oppressed go free, and that ye break every yoke?
7 Is it not to deal thy bread to the hungry, and that thou bring the poor that are cast out to thy house? when thou seest the naked, that thou cover him; and that thou hide not thyself from thine own flesh?
8 Then shall thy light break forth as the morning, and thine health shall spring forth speedily: and thy righteousness shall go before thee; the glory of the LORD shall be thy reward."

One dear sister decided to try this with all sincerity during her time of fasting. God had spoken to her and this is what she said: "I just want to thank you for helping me to get to the point to speak with Roger. Bishop, you have spoken to me about forgiveness (crying) while I was still angry with Roger even though we settled the issue. But I just could not let it go, so I'm asking God to forgive me for being angry and help me to truly forgive him. I just thank God for the prayers of the righteous. Thank you all for praying (sobbing)."

"Okay my sister" I responded "we understand, it is alright to cry. "Tears are a language that God understands." "The Psalmist writes 'weeping may endure for the night, but joy comes in the morning.' Your morning has come! This is God's way and it really works. Folks, this is what we call deliverance! And I want you to grasp it. This is what we call deliverance. Do not remain quiet, do not be afraid. It is about our eternal destiny. Do not fall into the trap of false security by saying well I am a Christian and I go to church. God wants you to live like He does because you are His child. The grace of God is sufficient to help you do what He wants you to do, forgive!"

Jesus admonished us in Luke 7:4 to Forgive even seven times in the same day. You have forgiven and God will honor you in this, but should offense come from the same offenders again, do not be distraught, apply Jesus' word and forgive again and again! It is not always easy to do so but God will give you the spiritual strength and grace to forgive, as you have been forgiven by Him.

Now take a moment and pray this prayer:

"O Lord my God, my heart yearns for more and more of You each day. Every time I try to reach up I feel pulled down by the memory of this pain I have been carrying. I truly want to forgive the ones who have offended me but I find it so hard. The wounds of their offense are still raw and open so I ask you to heal me, deliver me, free me, take this pain away and make me whole so I can forgive even as Jesus said, seven times in the ¢ame day. In Jesus name I pray. Amen!"

Chapter 2 Review

1. In addition to seven what is another sacred number?
2. Do you know of other facts that incorporates the number seven?
3. In extending forgiveness, is it wrong to bring up the past?
4. Deliverance comes to the one who offers forgiveness. Explain.
5. Can we avoid being offended? If not why not?
6. Write a prayer of forgiveness ten lines long.

Chapter 3

03

Seventy times Seven

The Silversmith holds the silver in the hottest part of the fire. You may be in the hottest part of the fire but remember that God, the Great Silversmith, is the One who is holding you! We are the silver He is refining.

Matthew 18:21-22
Then came Peter to him, and said, Lord, how oft shall my brother sin against me, and I forgive him? till seven times? [22] Jesus saith unto him, I say not unto thee, Until seven times: but, Until seventy times seven.

We slept in the church sanctuary at New Hope in East Windsor. Philip slept sitting in a chair on the platform and I slept on an air mattress. Jake and Israel slept on the floor. "It is not comfortable, trust me" said Philip. "In the past I used the air mattress bed but I'm not doing that this year I'm sleeping on a chair. There are beds I could sleep in but I'm trying to make a point this week and not be too comfortable and drift off into ease and forget the purpose of my mission and assignment from God for this week" he added.

I think that many of us have become really soft. I guess we forgot the days of all night prayer meetings, extended days of fasting: three days that could turn into five days and then to seven days. Some people I meet seem a bit surprised when they realize that some of us still fast for days on just water or fast a full day every week. One of my colleagues from another denomination was described as "old-school" because he fasted every Tuesday. I think the contemporary church has become too accustomed to luxury, finery and sophistication.

This reminds me of the response St. Thomas Aquinas gave to Pope Innocent II in the 13th century[4]. Displaying the ecclesiastical coffers the Pope said "see, Thomas, the church can no longer

---

[4] http://www.hymntime.com/tch/bio/a/q/u/aquinas_t.htm

say, Silver and gold have I none." Thomas Aquinas replied, "True, holy father, but neither can she now say, Rise up and walk." I hope we have not crossed the line and have become like the church of Pope Innocent II. It is my observation that we have become too comfortable and have forgotten some really important things.

One message of this book is for God to bring us back to our spiritual moorings. Mind you, nothing is wrong with prosperity and the enjoyment of it. But ever so often we need to "rough it" to remind ourselves of a dimension of Christianity so often forgotten these days. And that is SUFFERING! This also will help us to better identify with those who are suffering. Because we have literally become at ease in Zion, God allows us to experience pain and suffering through other means to sharpen us, purify us and make us into what He wants us to be. Frequently God allows that to occur through being offended over and over and having to forgive again and again. Seven Times? No! Seventy times Seven!

People who have achieved anything of significance in the Kingdom of God, does so with a story of pain and suffering. "No person can speak with such insight about human suffering without suffering himself.

Thomas Dexter Jakes has suffered greatly. He was 16 when his father died and became the provider for his mother and siblings. According to Atlantic Monthly, "Jakes said 'We lost everything.' 'I was literally cutting grass and digging ditches, trying to get diapers for my kids. So when I go into a home of somebody who doesn't have lights on, I've been there.' [5]

Oral Roberts lived in obscurity and poverty as a boy and almost died of tuberculosis at age 17.
Billy Graham was told that the most he could amount to was a poor preacher out in the sticks.
In 1967 Joni Eareckson Tada became paralyzed from the neck down at age 17.

William J. Seymour leader of the Azusa Street Revival that gave birth to the American Pentecostal Movement, was born in 1870 to former slaves Simon and Phyllis Salabar in Centerville, Louisiana.

The trajectory of the lives of the people God chooses to use is often punctuated with agony, discomfort and pain. Sometimes God allows us to

---

[5] http://etsministries.info/emails/TD.%20Jakes.htm

face trouble through what seems like calculated attacks by people we trusted. Some of these people are church people, family members, close friends, work-mates, school-mates, and sometimes even people we do not know.

The repeated attacks are like sand paper that is refining us, making us fit and useable to make something beautiful for God's use. Since sand paper was invented in China only in the 13th century, in order to make wood smooth for wooden products, the ancients used axes and saws to make boards from tree trunks. Next, they used adzes and chisels to smooth, shave and shape the planks for making fine furniture or beautiful sculpting. Finally, the wood was burnished in fire. These cutting tools and fire were used to process the wood. God allows us to be cut and chiseled, shaved, shaped and burnt by the offenses of life to make us better.

The Bible speaks clearly of the Refiner's fire in numerous places. Malachi 3:3 declares that God "will sit as a refiner and purifier of silver." The story is told of a silversmith who was asked when does he know that his silver is ready for use? In other words, when should he take the silver out of the fire? He answered 'when I can see my reflection[6] in it, then I know it is ready.'

The Silversmith holds the silver in the hottest part of the fire. You may be in the hottest part of the fire but remember that God, the Great Silversmith, is the One who is holding you! We are the silver He is refining. While we are being held in the hottest part of the fire, His eyes gaze steadfastly on us, He never looks away. He will not leave us longer than necessary in the fire. He will keep us there until the right moment, until we become the pure silver He desires and He can see Himself in us. Until there is the reflection or the image of God in and through our very lives and then and only then will He take us out of the fire because we will be ready for Him to use us. When God, the Great the Silversmith, sees a piece of jewelry on someone, He will know it is His silver because He will see His reflection in it. In addition, God, the Great Silversmith must have seen something worthy of his refining time and ability in the piece of raw silver that He selected to make a beautiful jewel. One day He will come to make up His jewels to adorn His bride, the Church, and the ones He refined will be prominent in His collection.

---

[6] http://www.clarion-call.org/extras/malachi.htm

Gold comes from gold ore that has been extracted from deep in the earth through blasting and digging. However, raw gold ore is not attractive and contains dirt and other impurities. In the ancient world, gold was purified through a three-stage process: crushing, washing and firing in a furnace. What the crushing left the washing removed and what the washing left the firing eradicated. Being made to go through the purification process is God's way of making us the best that we could be. Job said "when He hath tried me, I shall come forth as gold." (Job 23:10). It is not that God is willfully putting us in harm's way because He has a proclivity to sadism. He is our loving Father and He is also our Divine Goldsmith, He is purifying us for our good. When we are purified, we become beautiful and useful to our King.

The Biblical imagery illustrates the purification process in intricate details in the agricultural process. A three-stage process was employed: cutting, threshing and winnowing. For grain to be harvested from the fields the stalks are cut off, separated from the plants by the harvester. Next the harvested stalks are taken to the threshing floor. The threshing floor was usually a flat, hard, clay surface atop a hill where harvested stalks are brought to process the wheat, barley etc. To separate the grain from the stalk an ox would tread on the harvested stalk while dragging a thresher over the stalk. Eventually the grain is threshed or separated from the stalk but it remained on the threshing floor mixed into the shredded stalk and dust and dirt from the hard clay floor.

The next phase in the process was where a man, called the winnower, stands on the threshing floor on a windy evening and uses a winnowing fork, to pick up the mixture of grain, crushed stalk and dirt etc., and cast it into the air so the wind blows away the impurities called chaff and allow the pure grain to fall at the feet of the winnower. The winnowing process continues until the threshing floor is thoroughly purged of all impurities and the pure grain is on the floor. The Divine Harvester and Winnower[7] are purging our lives and one of the ways He does so, is by allowing us to be offended.

---

[7] [11] I indeed baptize you with water unto repentance. but he that cometh after me is mightier than I, whose shoes I am not worthy to bear: he shall baptize you with the Holy Ghost, and with fire: [12] Whose fan is in his hand, and he will throughly purge his floor, and gather his wheat into the garner; but he will burn up the chaff with unquenchable fire.

When we are offended, He expects us to forgive over and over and over again. God can prevent us from going through the pain of offense but He is processing us for His greater good. Pottery is one of the world's oldest crafts. Bowls, cups, and pots for the kitchen and roofing tiles, wall tiles and floor tiles, drain pipes, blocks and bricks were made of clay. There are three basic stages in making clay products, namely preparation, shaping and firing. Potters would work intensely crushing and kneading to have the best prepared clay for the shaping process. God sent Jeremiah the prophet down to the potter's house, and gave him a message. Jeremiah saw the potter working at the wheel. But the pot he was shaping from the clay was marred in his hands; so the potter formed it into another pot, shaping it as seemed best to him. Then the word of the LORD came to Jeremiah. God said, "Can I not do with Israel, as this potter does?" declares the LORD. "Like clay in the hand of the potter, so are you in my hand, Israel."

Jeremiah 18:1-6. Broken vessels are crushed, watered and reshaped. The perfection of the marred vessel is rooted in how well the clay is prepared. The process changes the consistency, viscosity and configuration of the clay until it is just right. This is done repeatedly making the clay ready for shaping into a vessel of honor. The more refined the clay the more valuable the vessel. Being compelled to face offense recurrently and made to forgive again and again, shapes us for God's use.

Space technology uses silica tiles[8] to cover the surface of Shuttles to facilitate reentry into the earth's atmosphere. Reentry exposes the space craft to temperatures that exceed 2500 degrees Fahrenheit. In the process of preparation these silica tiles are baked at temperatures that surpass 2300 degree Fahrenheit. The process makes the tiles ready to do their job of preventing the occupants of the shuttle from being burnt to death.

God prepares us like these silica tiles to prevent others from being plunged into the eternal fires of hell. Our preparation and purification often comes through having to forgive people over and over again. It is a long and painful process but we will shield many from hell-fire when we have been prepared by fire.

In Matthew 18 verse 21 Peter asked Jesus "Lord, how often shall my brother sin against me,

---

[8] http://www.airspacemag.com/how-things-work/shuttle-tiles-12580671/

and I forgive him? till seven times?" In verse 22 Jesus replied not "until seven times: but, Until seventy times seven." This encounter between Jesus and Peter takes place in the vicinity of the Mount of Transfiguration. Peter, James and John had just accompanied the Lord up to that Mountain and there they saw Jesus transfigured[9] or changed before their very eyes until His face shone like the sun and His clothing was turned into a glistening white light like no detergent or bleach could make it. The apostles were in awe but Jesus told them not to tell anyone what they had experienced until after the Lord had ascended to heaven. This brightness and the startling sight they beheld were to reveal to them the nature of purity by God's standard.

So when Peter asked the question, about the number of times he should forgive someone who offends him, shortly after the Transfiguration, his frame of reference was in synch with thorough purification of the soul until it became as pure as that of the Transfigured Christ he had just seen on the mountain. Peter wanted to be pure so he asked Jesus "Lord, how often shall my brother sin against

---

[9] And after six days Jesus taketh Peter, James, and John his brother, and bringeth them up into an high mountain apart, And was transfigured before them: and his face did shine as the sun, and his raiment was white as the light.

me, and I forgive him? till seven times?" After all seven is the number of perfection so it should suffice to attain Divine purification of the soul from all malice, bitterness and desires for revenge. Jesus surprised him by answering, "not until seven times, but until seventy times seven."

This command highlights God's desire for us to develop a disposition to forgiveness, a willingness to pardon and a character of compassion. These traits are not easily gendered nor are they automatically dispensed by the laying on of hands. These virtues are the products of multiple episodes of painful experiences generated in the fires of trials that come to make us strong. The trial of our faith[10] is designed to help us stretch and grow, break the barriers, think and function outside of the box, maneuver under fire and burn away sinful impurities from our lives until we come forth as purest gold.

Many people struggle with a recurrence of offenses from the same offenders. Here is a typical case to which we were asked to respond.

---

[10] That the trial of your faith, being much more precious than of gold that perisheth... 1 Peter 1:7(KJV)

"Good morning, thank you so much for raising this topic of forgiveness. It is something that I have been studying for a while and I am still seeking God for His forgiveness. I thank God for the moments of deliverance that I have had but I have a question for you, which is my personal struggle. How do you forgive when the person continues to do the same thing, exhibiting the same behavior?"

This is exactly what Jesus was addressing to Peter. "Not seven times, but seventy times seven."

Firstly, we have the God-given ability to forgive repeatedly. It is not impossible. It is unusual in our contemporary Christian culture; hence the very thought brings discomfort. We do not think in those terms. The mere fact that God brought it to you or allowed it to wind up on your door step is a clear indication that He knows you can handle it. You may not feel that way but you can handle it. Remember the process is designed to make you useable by God.

A key factor in changing directions is to realize that you are going the wrong way. It is time to make a U-turn. If this situation is making you miserable and you have built up a barrage of hurt and resentment toward the perpetrator until you are unable to function properly, you need deliverance. You are a marred or damaged pot and the Potter will need to break you to remake you, if you want Him to do so. This is tough stuff. It is not the feel-good stuff that burns up on reentry. When you go through God's refining fire you will be able to make it to where God wants you to go and you will bring some people along safely. As that offender repeats his or her negative behavior, your response is to forgive. God will give you the grace to do so. Our part is to forgive and ask God for His help.

One of the ways to start dealing with the situation is to stop talking about it. When the behavior continues remember Jesus' admonition to Peter, "seventy times seven." Jesus would never give that directive if He knew it was not possible for us to do. This is a tall order but God has it all charted out. 1 Corinthians 10: 13 (KJV) "There hath no temptation taken you but such as is common to man: but God is faithful, who will not suffer you to be tempted above that ye are able; but will with the temptation also make a way to escape, that ye may be able to bear it." God is faithful.

In other words, you need to come to the place where you believe that if God has brought you to it,

He will bring you through it. God always has a deliverance plan, an escape route or a parachute. God will never allow the devil to put on you or come your way or come at you, in a manner that you are not able to overcome it as a child of God. God has given you an escape route, there is a parachute somewhere there and our job is to find it.

[11]Growing up with my stepfather was very difficult at times. He was an alcoholic and his binges and daily bouts with rum, whisky, beer and whatever else he drank made him more difficult to live with as he grew older. I continued to forgive him. Eventually he began to see me in a different light. He realized that what I believed in was powerful and my Christianity was genuine. I grew up, got married and moved out. In 1989 my Mom died but I never cut him off and when he grew older I went to his rescue. I repaired his house and always did what I could to help him. I took him on a short vacation and told him that he needed to get right with God and give his heart to Jesus.

He did not do so right away but in 2004 one of my friends who pastored a church near my stepdad's house called me with the greatest news.

---

[11] Wayne Solomon's experience

"Your Dad gave his heart to the Lord, I led him to Jesus." It was a long and painful journey for me but forgiveness paid off in the end. I was at his bedside for the last days of his life in November 2009. He had asked for me to come when he realized he was dying. I did not hesitate, I just went to him. He could not speak but I spoke to him, shaved his face, tried to keep him comfortable. I kneeled at his bedside and prayed for him. All through life I forgave him every time he hurt me and I won in the end. Forgiveness works! I cannot tell you how your case will unfold, I cannot say if you will experience more or less pain and trouble than I did with the one who is hurting you but I can tell you, God will help you to become a forgiving person if you truly ask Him and when you forgive you too will win.

Read this prayer aloud.

"Our Father, I thank You for Your mercy. I give you the glory and honor and praise. I thank You for helping me to face my un-forgiveness. Lord for me this topic is heavy and the reality is that I am struggling with it. I ask You God to help me. I am not perfect but I am striving toward perfection. I look to You for help and ask Your forgiveness. As you know I have this scenario in my life and I need to forgive. I know I have hurt someone and I have been hurt intentionally or unintentionally. I ask You to forgive me Lord. Remove the unforgiving spirit from me. I pray dear God to be delivered from being buried under a sea of un-forgiveness. I decree and declare over my life that un-forgiveness is banished, I reject it and abandon it. Un-forgiveness is leaving and the Spirit of forgiveness, the Holy Spirit is working in my heart and making me a forgiving person that will obey Jesus and forgive Seventy times Seven, in Jesus name I pray. Amen!"

Chapter 3 Review

1. What do T.D Jakes, Joni Eareckson Tada and William J. Seymour have in common?
2. The processing of wheat, wood, clay, silver and gold teach what spiritual lessons?
3. When we repeatedly forgive someone and he or she continues to offend us how should we pray and act towards our offender?
4. Write your forgiveness story in 100 words or less.

Chapter 4

❧

Overcoming Obstacles to Forgiveness

"We represent our Heavenly Father when we forgive."

Matthew 18:3, 4, 5
³ And said, Verily I say unto you, Except ye be converted, and become as little children, ye shall not enter into the kingdom of heaven. ⁴ Whosoever therefore shall humble himself as this little child, the same is greatest in the kingdom of heaven. ⁵ And whoso shall receive one such little child in my name receiveth me.

"We glorify You Lord. We praise Your Holy Name. We thank You for the privilege you have given us that we can call upon Your Name. You are worthy of all glory and honor and praise and majesty. We ask You to move upon our hearts and teach us how to forgive as we accept Your forgiveness.

We ask that Your power will manifest to transform us. Thank You for the privilege of prayer in Jesus Name. Amen!"

My friend and his wife had been married for over twenty-five years when they agreed to file a divorce. He and I talked and prayed about it. I spoke with his wife. She was saddened by the prospect. She did not want her family to break up. The decree absolute was issued and they began the painful exercise of living separated.

No one really wins in a divorce and in my years as a Pastor, I have been to homes where arguments and even fist fights tore families apart, but un-forgiveness kept husbands and wives on the opposite sides of the fence at the expense of their children, their happiness and their love for each other. They built a firewall and repelled one another from their lives.

My friend called me one day and asked that I come over as he wanted to speak with me. I went over to his house and we sat in the living room. It was about their relationship. Eighteen months since he and his wife had been separated. He gave me the most exciting news I had heard from him in three years. His wife and he were getting back together.

Forgiveness is a conscious decision. They have chosen to leave the past behind and make a clean break from the desire to take revenge, to hate and to retaliate. They have forgiven each other. They are now ready to repair their family and restore, pardon, excuse, absolve, free and release each other.

When we forgive, we refuse to continue to hold or consider the offender guilty, though we may have been harmed or hurt willfully or inadvertently. When God forgives us, He justifies us or declares us righteous, just as if we had never sinned. Just think about what God has done for us. We broke God's laws, we have sinned against God, we transgressed His laws, we trespassed against Him. However, when we went to Him and asked Him to forgive us, He did. It is obvious that forgiveness does not occur or take place by osmosis. It must be deliberate, premeditated and calculated. We consciously must decide that we are going to forgive.

Forgiveness cannot happen by accident or coincidence. There must be intentionality to bring about forgiveness. You see the *natural* thing to do is not to forgive. Dr. Martin Luther King Jr discussed the nature of human behavior in this regard in his sermon on Love and Forgiveness[12]. The gist of King's message declares that if you think about it, our world itself, the world we live in, is not a forgiving place.

The whole culture is not a forgiving culture. If you don't pay your bills, your creditors will ensure that your credit score will be in ruins. If you don't pay your taxes the IRS can put you in prison. If you don't pay child-support the courts can put you in the jail house. Every public figure knows that the minute you make a mistake, there will be no shortage of opponents, who are ready and willing to drive the final nail into your coffin. You could do a million right things but the minute you do one thing wrong an avalanche of retribution and punishment is unleashed upon you. There is no forgiveness in Society. If you break the law they are going to arrest you.

Natural Laws taught us that there are consequences to our actions. If you jump off a roof the law of gravity will cause you to fall. If you touch fire you will be burned.

Un-forgiveness is a by-product of the fall of humanity. When humankind fell in the Garden of

---

[12] Love and Forgiveness http://www.thekingcenter.org/archive/document/love-and-forgiveness#

Eden, nature changed, and the environment became harsh and dangerous, humans changed and became vengeful and retaliatory, then un-forgiveness became the quintessential nature of the cosmos and of humanity. Forgiveness was unnatural. So, forgiveness does not and cannot happen naturally. People, society and nature itself just does not forgive. Forgiveness will only become natural when there is intentionality.

Remember, "Forgiveness is you willingly, excusing or pardoning the one who offends you." No one is forcing you to do this, you must do it voluntarily. You cannot even fake it. Genuine forgiveness cannot be counterfeited. To become a forgiving person, you must willingly give up your right to redress, retaliation and revenge. To forgive until it becomes a part of your nature takes work and Christ-like humility. To have a forgiving posture requires acquiring new attitudes.

Attitudes are habits of the mind. A forgiving lifestyle flows from new attitudes generated in a renewed mind. Forgiveness will help you to unload the weight and burden of resentment. When you have forgiven, you will be free from resentment towards someone who has wronged you, regardless of how painful that wrong might have been. What you are actually saying then is "I have stopped holding this thing in my heart. I understand that I have been hurt but I gave up my right to retaliate. I let that person go free." This is the only way if we want the world to be a better place. The world continues in a state of un-forgiveness. Relatively few people are practicing forgiveness, because most people really find it difficult to forgive. There are several reasons why un-forgiveness persists. These obstacles block the doors of our hearts and prohibit us from forgiving.

Forgiveness Overcomes Pride

The number one issue is pride. Someone may think, "You cannot do that to me and just walk away. You need to pay." Pride is a big problem. Matthew 18 is a powerful chapter that deals with forgiveness. Usually, in studying forgiveness there are some obvious verses exegeted, but if you look carefully, you will see that from the very beginning, the chapter highlights how pride is nuanced, to pervert and prevent forgiveness. The disciples asked Jesus who is greatest in God's Kingdom. Surely, they did not anticipate His answer.

Jesus called a little child and set him in the middle of them, and said, "except you be converted, and become as little children, you shall not enter the kingdom of heaven. Whoever shall humble himself as this little child is the greatest in the kingdom of heaven. And whoever shall receive one such little child in my name receives me." (Matthew 18:1-5)

A little child? A young child? The word used here for child is from the Greek word transliterated, *paidion* phonetically spelt *pahee-dee'-on*. This word is a neuter gender noun that means a little child, an infant, *a child under training*. This infers a *teachable person, a person who can be molded or shaped by the Teacher*. The greatest in the Kingdom of heaven are like little children. You see how children behave. They have conflict and offend one another but they do not hold on to their hurt. They may pout for a few minutes but they go right back and play with the same kid that hurt them. They have no pride! This is exactly what Jesus expects of us. To enter any Kingdom, you must know the rules of the Kingdom.

The principal rule of the Kingdom of Heaven is forgiveness. God let us into His Kingdom via the door of forgiveness and He expects us to have a disposition to forgiveness, holding no malice or desire for revenge, having no pride just like teachable children. In Matthew 18:3 Jesus explained that to enter the Kingdom of Heaven, you must be *converted* and become as little children. Note the word converted comes from a Greek word that means to *turn, to change direction, or go the other way.* The world goes the way of un-forgiveness, you need to go the other way, about face, turn around and forgive! You will become free from the desire to take revenge.

The problem that people face when they are unwilling to forgive is generated by an attitude of pride. Pride is at the root of it. Pride is the problem. People feel the need to lash out and to retaliate. They either fight or take flight. People decide to fight because of pride. Understand that it is a reaction; just responding because of how you felt at the moment you were wronged. No one is denying what was done to you was wrong. What happened to you was unfair. That's legitimate. But really it is not what happens to you but how you choose to respond to what has happened will shape your life forever. Yes, how you choose! You decide, you choose how you plan to respond. You determine what to do after the seed of offense has been planted in your garden. You decide whether you will water it with pride or you will smother it with forgiveness. If you respond with pride then you will not want to forgive the person who wronged you. Un-forgiveness will create bitterness.

In some instances, you may respond wrongly at the moment, but when you get over the initial trauma you will need to set your course. Dr. Fedlyn Beason says it like this "It does not matter how contrary the winds blow, what matters is how you set your sail."[13] Be like the little children, forgive quickly and overcome pride.

Forgiveness Overcomes Bitterness

Bitterness is another obstacle to forgiveness. Once bitterness gets into the picture it will just keep generating more un-forgiveness. The more bitter a person feels the more likely they are to refrain from forgiveness.

Bitterness, by definition, *is drinking poison and hoping the other person dies*. You drink the poison and hope the person who offended you falls over and dies. I can tell you right now they are not

---

[13] Dr. Fedlyn Beason: Educator, Administrator, Minister of the Gospel

going to die but you will become so toxic from un-forgiveness that you will die! This is what un-forgiveness does. When people hold on to un-forgiveness they think they are punishing the other person, but more often than not, they themselves are being punished. You lose relationships; you lose freedom, because bitterness weighs you down. If you find yourself talking about it all the time, if you recognize that you make every opportunity to bring it up, if you notice that the moment that person's name comes up you are ready to talk about the same incident that happened 20 years ago, 20 months ago, it means that you are fixated on it because you have not forgiven and you are still bitter. Since bitterness hurts the one that is bitter, it is best to get rid of the bitterness in order to live liberated, so forgive! God wants you to let bitterness go by forgiving. You may not forget what happened right away but in time, you will be able to cope with the memories and you will heal because you let the person go.

Forgiveness Overcomes Anger

Anger is a strong feeling of annoyance, displeasure, or hostility. It is the basis for much of the violence in our world. People get angry and this can lead to un-forgiveness which maintains a disposition to anger. Anger is displayed in our culture through negative behaviors such as road rage and domestic violence that claims the lives of almost 40% of the women murdered in America every year. To diffuse anger, forgiveness must take place. Turning the other cheek, walking away, counting to ten, taking deep breaths are all techniques used to suppress anger. However, anger born of un-forgiveness will only dissipate when the offended chooses to forgive. People can get angry and stay angry for a lifetime. When anger rises, it is hard to control. The Bible says in Ephesians 4:26 "Don't let the sun go down on your wrath." The remedy for overcoming anger from offense is to forgive.

Forgiveness and Trust

We talked about overcoming pride, bitterness and anger. Sometimes forgiveness depends on the willingness to trust again. Someone may say, "Because you hurt me I would not, do not and cannot trust you. I do not think I could ever trust you again so I do not want to have anything to do with you."

In close relationships like marriage, the trust factor is huge. Unfaithfulness to marital vows is severely painful. Your spouse may reveal some past failures, or some secret event. Then you know for sure that you have actually been offended and you find it so hard to forgive because you do not trust him/her anymore. You figure that if you forgive them, then you open yourself to be hurt again. So, the way people deal with this is to refuse to forgive because if they truly forgive, they think they will be expected to trust again and that is so very hard.

Forgiveness will help us, in time to trust again. Past experiences destroy trust and the unwillingness to trust can sometimes prevent forgiveness. This is a bitter pill to swallow and no one expects you to readily accept these concepts.

You can forgive even though you are not able to trust your offender again. I guess the power of love will eventually prevail in gendering forgiveness and trust. 1Corinthians 13 reveals the anatomy of love. It says in verse 5, "[14]Love keeps no record of wrongs!" Remember Christ Jesus Himself on the cross, He said "Father forgive them for they know not what they do[15]." Jesus did not

---

[14] Love is patient, love is kind. It does not envy, it does not boast, it is not proud. [5] It does not dishonor others, it is not self-seeking, it is not easily angered, it keeps no record of wrongs. [6] Love does not delight in evil but rejoices with the truth. [7] It always protects, always trusts, always hopes, always perseveres.
[15] Luke 23: 34

68

just teach forgiveness, He did not just preach it. He lived it! He forgave everyone, everything!

Think about Jesus and Judas. Jesus had knowledge that Judas had betrayed Him yet the same night Jesus washed Judas' feet, He forgave him even before Judas performed his evil act. Knowing the pain, the shame, the reproach, the humiliation and the agony, Jesus even gave Judas communion. "This is My body broken for you Judas. This is my blood shed for you Judas. I am going to die for you Judas. I still love you Judas though I know you have already betrayed Me." Someone may have betrayed you, will you forgive them? They betrayed your trust, they betrayed your love, and they betrayed your confidence. Will you, could you ask God to help you forgive them? This is not easy but God expects us to forgive and He will help us to do so. Forgiveness helps to overcome the unwillingness to trust.

Forgiveness Overcomes Offenses caused by a Lack of Knowledge

Another major barrier to forgiveness is the lack of knowledge. Sometimes someone may say something or do something and you get hurt. That person had no intention to hurt you and did not realize you could be hurt, but you got hurt.

Further, someone may have carried out an instruction from a superior or responded to a situation and you became the *collateral damage.* Sometimes a person might have been manipulated or used by someone else and you felt they were doing it to you on purpose but they were innocent. You did not know so you blame them for hurting you and refused to forgive them.

Another aspect of the lack of knowledge is when you do not have all the information. You do not know what really happened. You do not know why the person behaved in such a manner. They may have mental issues[16] that just began to surface. They may have been hurt by someone else and you become the object of their misguided retaliation. It is so complex at times.

In addition, without the knowledge or being misinformed there is the tendency to not forgive. Further, people feed the rumor mill and traffic in gossiping, especially through social media these days, so you need to find out for yourself. Some people just like to take some truth, mix it with lies

[16] 26.2% of Americans over 18 have some form of mental disorder.
http://www.thekimfoundation.org/html/about_mental_ill/statistics.html

and peddle that poison to cause division. That is the working of the devil in and through those people. They will take something from one person and tell it to another person who they know will be hurt by it just to stir up trouble. You find those kinds of people in schools, on the job, in churches etc.

A forgiving disposition will spare us from hurting when we have little or no knowledge in these situations. I know forgiving is not always easy but forgive your offender, leave her or him to God.

"Dear God of heaven and earth, my heart is so broken from the many offenses I have suffered. I do not want to be an unforgiving person but that is exactly where I am right now. The way I feel is that I want the one who offended me to pay or be punished for what they did to me. I really don't want to remain that way so I am asking you to change my heart. I am asking You to change my attitudes. Help me to stop talking about my hurt. Help me to think of You and Your love for me demonstrated by Your Son, Jesus, on the Cross. Lord show me if I have been offended by someone who had no knowledge that they hurt me, or by someone who was used to hurt me. Lord I release my offender, I put them in

Your merciful hands and pray like Jesus, "Father forgive them for they know not what they do." And Lord in the process heal me from holding pride, anger, bitterness, and unwillingness to trust again. I receive Your forgiveness and I forgive my offender in Jesus name. Amen!"

Chapter 4 Review

1. Why is forgiveness described as unnatural?
2. List the barriers to forgiveness in order—from most difficult to easiest to change.
3. Explain how bitterness develops and how to get rid of it.
4. Marriages dissolve every day because of infidelity. Discuss why infidelity is so difficult to forgive and how couples who have forgiven each other accomplished it.

Chapter 5

⟨image⟩

Forgiveness is an A C T

"Keep your eyes on God, not the offender."

Proverbs 28:13 "He that covers his sins shall not prosper: but whoso confesses and forsakes them shall have mercy."

"December 2016 dawned on us in the Mid Atlantic without much ado. The temperatures of the frigid winter days, did not register the Arctic freeze and blustering storms, to which we had all become accustomed, during the last five years. My mother was coming to visit for two weeks, so the mild winter would better suit her.   But I was not comfortable and for the first time in years I dreaded Christmas.

My mother and I never had a good relationship. Mom divorced my stepfather when my sister and I were quite young, and worked over time as a police officer to make ends meet. My mother taught me how to be respectful and well-mannered but at the same time, she taught me fear by abusing me mentally, emotionally and physically. I wanted so much to love and trust her, but deep inside I prayed for God to take me. After I moved away to pursue my studies I would make brief trips home to visit my family and friends. December 24, 2016, arrived and so did Mom. She was there to spend Christmas with my husband, our children and me.

We managed to make it through Christmas and a few days later, a dear friend sent me a note to listen to New Hope Church of God Senior Pastor, Bishop Philip M. Bonaparte's playback. Pastor and his guest Pastor Wayne C. Solomon were teaching a series on "Forgiveness from the Heart." I froze as they discussed "Forgiveness as a deliberate decision to release someone who has harmed, hurt or violated you." I remembered studying Matthew 6:12 and Mark 11:25. The pastors further confirmed it was my duty as a Christian to forgive; otherwise bitterness and anger would enter my heart. That's exactly how I felt.

All my life, I strived to walk in the ways of the Lord, but the bitterness in my heart towards my mother always felt like a spiritual weight. In the back of my mind, I always knew I had to find a way to forgive and honor my mother, 'the first commandment with promise.'

I joined the New Hope Prayer Line over the next few days, twice daily as the pastors prayed and fasted at New Hope in New Jersey. The teachings were powerful.

I learned that forgiveness required action; ACT: A admission, C confession and T transformation, (how I behave following forgiveness). This was going to be the answer to my prayer. I was determined to create a culture of forgiveness for my life. After listening to the prayer line recordings several times, I felt a powerful stirring up in my chest and a strong urge to forgive my mother for the years of abuse and pain I had endured. I felt that my walk with God and even my salvation depended on forgiving my mother.

I remember walking up to her on New Year's Eve not knowing what I was going to say or what to expect from her. I opened my mouth and it was as if the Spirit of the Lord spoke through me. The next words I said aligned with what the Holy Spirit wanted me to say. I heard myself saying, "Mommy, I forgive you for everything you have ever done to me." My mother became furious and started swearing at me. She talked about being a single parent, doing the best she could, but did not admit to any wrongdoing. As my mother continued to swear at me, I asked her to forgive me for anything I did to hurt her and I told her that I loved her with the love of God.

She became silent and did not respond. It didn't matter that she had been shouting and swearing at me in the front yard of our home, I felt a weight lifted from me at the very moment I said 'I FORGIVE YOU.'

Later that night I joined the Prayer Line and heard Pastors Bonaparte and Solomon likening forgiveness from the heart to open heart surgery. It takes time to heal. Although my mother became withdrawn and reserved, I was rejoicing in my spirit. I was free at last to serve the Lord in spirit and in truth. On New Year's Day, I blessed and anointed my family, and with my mother's permission blessed her as well. I asked her to bless me, which she did, wondering 'how could my daughter ask me to bless her when I am not speaking to her.' I offered the bottle of olive oil to her. She said 'thank you' and took the bottle of oil, anointed me and blessed me.

I received that maternal blessing with joy. It was the seal of the healing that I received when I told her, 'I forgive you.' It soothed all the years of pains I had endured.

A week after my mother returned home, she began calling me just to say 'hello.' She called me a few days ago, to invite our children to spend the summer with her. Our conversations have been very pleasant and cordial. I have no anxiety or stress when I think of her. Yesterday my mother sent me a text message, "Praise God for His mercy." I am thankful that nothing is impossible with God." [17]

---

[17] *Testimony of a New Hope Prayer-line Member.*

Forgiveness is an ACT
The bible says in Proverbs 28:13 "He <u>that covers his sins shall not prosper</u>: but whoso confesses and forsakes them shall have mercy."
Forgiveness is an ACT: Admission, Confession, Transformation!

A for Admission. Admission means to refuse to cover the sin of un-forgiveness any longer. You must admit. Realize that there is a problem. Admit "I have a problem, something I have not cleaned up." When a person's mental, emotional, spiritual or physical health is impaired by un-forgiveness, they must come to the place of recognizing and exposing the problem, by admitting to themselves and others that they have a problem. When un-forgiveness genders a vengeful attitude, sin begins to take root in the heart. Drug addicts, alcoholics, porn addicts all must admit they have a problem before they can get help to recover. They must ADMIT. So too the person steeped in un-forgiveness, must admit that there is a problem for which God's help is needed.

C for Confession is the next step in being healed from un-forgiveness. Proverbs 28:13 "He that covers his sins shall not prosper: but whoso <u>confesses</u> and forsakes them shall have mercy." Confession begins with confession to God. 1 John 1:9 "If we confess our sins, he is faithful and just to forgive us our sins, and to cleanse us from all unrighteousness." James 5:16 "<u>Confess</u> your faults one to another, and pray one for another, <u>that ye may be healed</u>...." Confession brings healing to the one who confesses (the offended), to the one to whom the confession is made (the offender) and to the body as a whole.

Finally, **T is for Transformation**. Proverbs 28:13 "He that covers his sins shall not prosper: but whoso confesses and <u>forsakes them</u> shall have mercy." Transformation means I must be changed. Forsake, abandon, jettison the old behaviors, be transformed so that you think and act differently. Romans 12:2 "And be not conformed to this world: but <u>be ye transformed by the renewing of your mind</u>, ..." Transformation takes place as a renewal or change of heart and life is achieved by God's power.

The habits of your mind or your attitudes, will be changed by the power of God, as you read and study the word of God consistently. When attitudes are transformed, behaviors will change. You will think and act differently towards the one who offended you and you will experience TRANSFORMATION.

Forgivingness means not holding your offender as wrong anymore, even though they did wrong. When God forgives you no matter how much you sinned, your slate is wiped clean and you get to start from scratch again. That's what God wants to do through you. He wants you to be able to treat your offender that you forgive as He treats us. "Forgive us our trespasses as we forgive those who trespass against us." Do not remain fixated on your offender, let your heart be fixed on God, put your faith in God, put your trust in God.

Fixate on the promises of God and soon you will realize, the burden you have been carrying has been lifted. This is a difficult issue for many people but the principles for its resolution, is the same as in any situation where you feel overwhelmed, outgunned or outnumbered by the enemy. Let's take a look at a story in the life of Jehoshaphat as recorded in II Chronicles 20.

A three-nation confederacy invaded Judah and was bent on attacking and destroying Jerusalem.

Jehoshaphat prayed in II Chronicles 20:12 saying, "our God, wilt thou not judge them? for we have no might against this great company that cometh against us; neither know we what to do: <u>but our eyes are upon thee</u>." In other words, "I trust you God."

It may take a long time to be able to trust the offender again but your focus should be on trusting God not the offender. When we forgive someone, we have to trust God to take care of the details. God will take care of the restoration, the renewal of our hearts and our lives. God will also take care of the retribution for what has happened to you.

Like Jehoshaphat, keep your eyes on God not the offender. In fact, if your offender is sincere and remorseful he or she may never pay for what they did to you, because God is merciful. He has mercy on whoever He desires to have mercy on. That does not mean that the person's wrongs have not been punished. Jesus was punished for what that person did to you. Jesus paid for all the sins of the world on the cross of Calvary. Retribution took place already. Your sins and mine have also been judged and paid for by Christ. Engage in the ACT of forgiveness!

Pray this prayer aloud!

"Lord I approach Your Holy presence, I thank You today for who You are and what You have done for us. I thank You Holy Spirit for Your presence. I ask You to illuminate me, to light me up, to sanctify me, consecrate me, lift me up and fill me up. Fill me with Your unconditional love in the Name of Jesus, love for others, love for You in Jesus Name. I ask you dear Lord, sweet Holy Spirit, Heavenly Guide, lead me in Your path of resplendent light. Anoint me with Your oil of gladness and make my life fragrant. O Sweet Fragrance of Heaven, Jesus Son of God, Lover of my soul. Lord as I enter the Holy of Holies, I am reminded that You sit on the mercy seat, so I thank You for giving me mercy, even as I am merciful to others and as I forgive them, for Your Son's sake, in Jesus Name. Amen."

Chapter 5 Review

1. What does the acronym A C T stand for?
2. In the story of the woman and her mother, the daughter went the extra mile. Are you willing to go the extra mile? Share your story of forgiveness.
3. "Our eyes are upon You Lord." Discuss this statement in reference to forgiveness.

Chapter 6

❧

Transforming
a Culture of Un-forgiveness

"... Forgiveness is the attribute of the strong."
Mohandas Gandhi

2 Timothy 1:7, 'For God hath not given us the spirit of fear; but of power, and of love, and of a sound mind.'

Taylor had worked for an international organization for over 35 years and was in line for an executive level position. Her mentor, Lacey, and close friend, an upper level executive, had been like an older sister to her for nearly two decades. Their families had become very close to one another as well.

Lacey told Taylor to fire a subordinate but Taylor did not want to do it, as the subordinate had done nothing that warranted dismissal. Taylor wrestled with the matter and eventually let Lacey know she would not comply. Lacey retaliated with virulent fury. She turned on Taylor, broke off their long-standing relationship and engineered a plan to have Taylor assigned to a lower paying job in another location that was very far from her home and family. Taylor felt betrayed, violated and used. She had worked with Lacey for most of her adult life helping Lacey to achieve her dreams. Now Lacey just pulled the rug from under her, embarrassed her and ruined her opportunity to be promoted in the company. Taylor's heart became saturated with a desire to see Lacey hurt and thought of ways Lacey could be made to pay.

Lacey was wrong but Taylor's immediate response was to see Lacey punished for what she did to her. Taylor was not quick to forgive, she was quick to repay. Taylor's behavior is typical in a culture of un-forgiveness.

If someone wrongs us, we see their faults and ignore our own to justify our negative disposition for revenge. Why have we become so prone to revenge? Why is there no natural desire to heal? Why is there rather an unnatural desire to hurt? Why has our world become so callous?

Our world has become so accustomed to revenge, retribution, vindication and retaliation, that when forgiveness takes place it seems like an anomaly. We use revenge as a means of solving our problems and obviously, it has not worked so we live in a toxic culture of un-forgiveness. Cultures the world over maintain the system of an eye for an eye.

Every culture on this planet is punitive and retributive. Retributive Justice is the system of law that has characterized and governed Western culture for millennia. Sadly, this system is not effective in the reduction of crime rates. From 1970 to 2005[18] there was a 700% increase in the United States [19]prison population. Then by the year 2015, the incarcerated population was 2,173,800 prisoners in the United States or about 22% of the world's prison

---

[18] "After a 700-percent increase in the US prison population between 1970 and 2005, you'd think the nation would finally have run out of lawbreakers to put behind bars," said the report by Pew's Public Safety Performance Project.

[19] http://www.dailykos.com/story/2007/2/15/302239/-

population[20], while America is just about 4.4% of the world's population.[21]

Incarceration increases because society requires that all crime be punished and law breakers be incarcerated. The only response by society is retaliation. Society is un-forgiving. In the world of organized crime and street gangs, retaliation and revenge for so-called honor have snuffed out far too many innocent lives. Wars, the destroyer of millions of lives, often stem from revenge or the desire to punish for infraction. The entire world will obviously benefit if there is a paradigm shift from a culture of un-forgiveness to a forgiveness culture.

Culture is defined as a way of living. Beliefs, norms, values, language, symbols and technology are the elements of culture. Norms are rules or guidelines for behaviors a given society considers acceptable. Un-forgiveness is a prevailing norm of contemporary society. It is manifested in physiological problems, hate, fear, desire to hurt or see the offender hurt and paranoia.

In a culture of un-forgiveness, paranoia poisons the lives of disproportionate numbers of

---

[20] https://www.bjs.gov/index.cfm?ty=pbdetail&iid=5870
[21] https://www.census.gov/popclock/

people. For example: Adolf Hitler suffered from paranoia as seen in his constant psychological projections. Hitler convinced the German population that their problems were all attributable to the Jews living in the Rhineland. His paranoia was soon extended to include Gypsies, Communists, Socialists and Protestants.

Nativism, a policy of protecting the interests of native-born residents, against those of immigrants: and Xenophobia, or the fear of strangers, characterized German society as most of the German population believed that the groups who were singled out, had offended them and deserved to be punished. Ultimately these practices brought the demise and destruction of Germany, when the Allied forces of the Second World War defeated the Third Reich. Today we see a resurgence of nationalism, nativism and xenophobia in numerous countries of our world. Hate groups engaged in spewing projection rhetoric are drawing the attention of a naïve citizenry. Un-forgiveness is in the DNA of this paranoia as nativists truly believe, they have been wronged by outsiders and that they need to take revenge. They are not inclined to forgive for perceived wrong-doing because un-forgiveness is the cultural norm.

Physical and Emotional Transformation

In a culture of un-forgiveness, physiological impairment as coronary diseases, hypertension, stress, strokes, acid reflux and ulcers, become prevalent. In addition, characteristic of a culture of un-forgiveness include a preponderance of psychological problems.

In my practice as a physician, I have come across cases where un-forgiveness was at the root of physical problems. Such was the case of a man who had been rushed into the emergency room where I worked as a physician. He was having a heart episode and could not function at his job. After treating him I learned that his boss had made it difficult for him at his workplace. Because of un-forgiveness he harbored anger and bitterness until it led to his coronary condition.

His healing would come after he decided to forgive his boss and let the matter go. It did not happen overnight but as he prodded through the process both his emotional and physical conditions improved.

Healing for a wounded Heart

Hate is the currency of a culture of un-forgiveness and it can consume a person like it did Jana. "My father and my stepmom abused me for as long as I could remember," said Jana, a faithful church member. "As I grew older and the abuse persisted and increased, I got sick and began to lose weight. The torment and torture inflicted on me filled me with bitter hate. They had wronged me for so long that when I thought of them I could taste the hate in my mouth. I moved away but hate for them continued to saturate my life. After many years, I felt impelled by the Holy Spirit to forgive my father.

My father came to visit me and I mustered up the courage to approach him. I went to him and said 'Daddy, I forgive you.' He responded in a manner I did not expect. 'I am sorry for all we did to you Jana. I had no idea you suffered that much.' I felt a healing deep inside and all the hate in my heart vanished. My father died two weeks later.

I am grateful to God that I had the opportunity to let him know that I forgave him and be healed from hate." Jana now lives at peace with herself and is filled with love and not hate because she forgave.

Overcoming Fear

In a culture of un-forgiveness, fear or phobias are pervasive. In the United States, Psychologists have identified about 500 phobias suffered by some 50 million Americans. After the fear of failure and the fear of death, the fear of rejection is the next strongest fear among humans. Many people do not approach their offenders to offer forgiveness because they fear being rejected. Don't fear what the offender may think or do, following your offer of forgiveness.

You may be surprised to find out that the offender was anxiously waiting to fix things with you. Overcoming the fear of rejection will result in reconciliation when forgiveness is given and received.

Reena is a highly-educated woman that is respected by her family, church and community. She was very reluctant to take the first step, on the road to forgiving those who had offender her. For one thing, she felt since she was in the right, keeping her distance as she had been doing was the correct way to handle offenders. In addition, she was afraid her offenders may reject her offer of forgiveness.

Notwithstanding, after viewing the forgiveness series on Facebook she felt the need to forgive. "I have a list of nine people I need to forgive," she told us. She began working on her list because God was dealing with her and she wanted to fix things. She faced her fear armed with 2Timothy 1:7, 'For God hath not given us the spirit of fear; but of power, and of love, and of a sound mind.' Obviously, anxiety can well up in your chest, when you make the call. Your breathing may alter and you will need to pause and take a couple deep breaths. "To overcome the fear of rejection the offended person needs to deprogram," said Reena. By this she means; unravel the tightly wound strands of nervous, anticipatory thoughts of a negative outcome, fill your heart with love for the offender and expect that God's power will fix the things we cannot. Reena testified to us of her healing, "I called six people and got up the nerve to say 'I forgive you.'" When we forgive, it heals us as it did for Reena.

Fragrance of Forgiveness

Working in a San Francisco flower-shop, may seem to be a gentle pleasant job, filled with the beauty and fragrance that fresh blossoms from around the world, could bring each employee every day. However, it was not so for Haley, a young female Christian florist, who had worked there for a while. Haley was stunned one day to discover Jenkins had told a terrible lie on her that caused her appalling grief, humiliation and embarrassment.

"I began to internalize the pain of the offense until my prayer to God was to do something to Jenkins for what he had done to me. 'Kill him God, kill him or move him,' became my daily petition. Things got worse and worse but God continued to urge me, to do what I knew was right. I went to Jenkins and held him by the hands. With the deepest sincerity, I could muster, I said 'Please forgive me,' I told him how sorry I was, for how I thought and felt about him. 'Also, I want you to know that I forgive you for what you did to me.' Things changed between us, and for me, the flower-shop became perfumed with the fragrance of forgiveness. I truly now understand, the words of the Apostle Paul found in Ephesians 4:32 '...be ye kind one to another, tenderhearted, forgiving one another, even as God for Christ's sake hath forgiven you.'"

Why are we desensitized to others who are hurting? Why is there no compassion toward our sisters and brothers? Of course, there are many reasons but media stands out as a noteworthy culprit. Media has injected humanity with this numbness of desensitization. Television broadcast, radio and printed news for example, have become more graphic, crude and desacralized over the last fifty years. Human tragedy and pain are exposed to public view. Nothing is sacred, tabooed or kept confidential anymore. Privacy is a relic of the past and its companion, decency vanished decades ago from the media. Reality shows, now the ratings booster for all networks, have a no holds barred, unchained, unshackled, uncensored approach to entertainment. The private lives of ordinary citizens have been turned into public spectacle.

The aftermath of life after the shows is tragic, catastrophic and heart-breaking, to say the least in many cases. Some of these former reality stars have jumped to their deaths or took overdoses and died.

The uncompassionate demeanor of contemporary society has no doubt also been cut from the cloth of the world of violent video games. These games show no respect for life itself. The annihilation of tens of thousands of characters; alien or animal, cartoon or human proceeds with numbing ease, without mourning, grief or shock. Kill, kill, kill him or kill her are bloodletting mantras that are droned onto the underdeveloped, naïve brains of ten-year-old children, that are glued to controllers from which laser beams, side-winder missiles, torpedoes, bullets, rockets and the like are fired relentlessly. We are numb, as accurately described in the 2006 U2, lyrics of the hit-song NUMB[22]:

"I feel numb,
I feel numb,
Too much is not enough,
I feel numb."

In addition, we are confused because of the blurring of reality with fantasy. Movies of the sci-fi ilk are not the sole purveyors of this confusion but in every genre; from children's movies, where cartoon characters and humans, conduct steamy romances, to alien wars, where mere mortals are transformed into mayhem making machines that defeat and oust alien invaders; from culinary competitions, where chefs are pitted against each other to create pleasant provisions, to political

---

[22] https://www.last.fm/music/U2/_/Numb+(The+Soul+Assassins+Mix)/+lyrics

enterprises that traffic in hyperbole and create false narratives for political traction; truth is a rare commodity. No wonder we are numb. No wonder we are uncompassionate. No wonder our world is characterized by a culture of un-forgiveness.

The operating system of such a culture is evil. It pervades thought and action. So regardless of the medium, the application or the objective, evil is the underlying factor. It is the sauce, the seasoning, the atmosphere, the environment, the temperature, the texture, the generator and disburser of human expression. It controls and coordinates, calculates and computes actions and reactions, behaviors and responses. Fault begets retribution. Hurt elicits reprisal. Misconduct genders revenge. Transgression seeds retaliation. Trespass provokes payback. Wrongdoing produces punishment and offense brings un-forgiveness.

Such a culture is in need of transformation and it must begin with each of us through Christ-like forgiveness.

"Dear Lord I truly want to expel un-forgiveness from my heart. There are so many things about my life that have been tragically affected by un-

forgiveness. I ask You to send the power of Your Spirit into my life and overpower every trace of un-forgiveness in me. I give myself freely to you to be an ambassador of Your forgiveness to our world that constantly seeks revenge. Help me in even a small way to impart to someone Your compassionate love. Heal our world of un-forgiveness. Purge our world of the desire for revenge. Cleanse our world of the disposition to retribution and give us a passion to pardon, an excitement to excuse and a capacity to be compassionate and forgiving, like Christ our Lord, in Jesus Name. Amen!

Chapter 6 Review

1. List the indicators of a culture of un-forgiveness.
2. Discuss the physiological manifestations of un-forgiveness.
3. Explain how hate is overcome.
4. Discuss the desensitized nature of our culture.

Chapter 7

∝

A Culture of Forgiveness

"Love is the lubricant, engine and operating system of heaven. Heaven's very character, nature and culture harks of love. The entire environment is saturated with the presence of God"

Ephesians 4:32 "And be ye kind one to another, tenderhearted, forgiving one another, even as God for Christ's sake hath forgiven you"

On Wednesday June 17, 2015 when 21-year-old Lexington County South Carolina native, Dylan Roof, entered the Historic Emanuel AME Church in Charleston, and sat next to one of the women there for Bible Study. No one knew what he had on his mind. He reloaded his gun, five times and fatally shot nine parishioners including the Pastor, Clementa Pinckney.

His plan was to begin a race war between African-Americans and White Americans. This backfired on Roof as the African-Americans and their White sisters and brothers joined hands and defied hate and racism. The family members of the victims chose to forgive Roof and not seek revenge. "I forgive you," the daughter of victim Ethel Lance, 70, said to Roof, "You took something very precious from me and I will never talk to her ever again. I will never be able to hold her again. But I forgive you. And have mercy on your soul." At the sentencing of Dylan Roof, on January 12, 2017, the relatives of victims passionately pleaded with an expressionless Roof, who never made eye contact, to ask God's forgiveness and turn to Christ. The Emmanuel AME Church had created a culture of forgiveness and showed the society a powerful example of it.

A Culture of Forgiveness will crush the prevailing cultural patterns and destroy the established practices of our societies that are held captive in the clutches and grasp of un-forgiveness.

Indicators of a Culture of Forgiveness

Such a culture will be transformational. Be reminded of the words of the Apostle Paul:

"I beseech you therefore, brethren, by the mercies of God, that ye present your bodies a living sacrifice, holy, acceptable unto God, which is your reasonable service. 2 And be not conformed to this world: but be ye transformed by the renewing of your mind, that ye may prove what is that good, and acceptable, and perfect, will of God." (Romans 12:1-2 (KJV))

Verse 2 says, "do not be like the world." Do not adapt to the culture of the world. Do not be shaped by the world. Do not let the world squeeze you into its mold. It is like taking putty and making molded objects. The writer, Paul, is saying do not be conformed but be transformed.

Remember, forgiveness is an ACT: Admission, Confession and Transformation. One of the evidences that we have forgiven, that we have the spirit of forgiveness, is that we are transformed. Our disposition to forgiveness will be seen in our willingness to forgive and pardon repeatedly.

Forgiving without limit until it is almost automatic, natural and normal, until it becomes a norm or the socially acceptable behavior in society, will signal that we are practicing a culture of forgiveness because we have been transformed.

But how do you do that? How does an individual get transformed? How do you go from being un-forgiving in nature, in a world inundated with retribution and retaliation, being its essence, to being a forgiving restorative person? How does one experience cultural transformation?

My brother is an Organization Development Consultant. He helps organizations develop strategies and cultures for greater effectiveness and efficiency. These entities must experience Cultural Transformation to become more successful. By taking a holistic look at entities to determine where they are and discovering their desired destination, a consultant can chart a course in that direction. What exactly does a culture of forgiveness look like? What are the beliefs, norms, values and language?

The best ways to know about a culture are to visit the place where the practitioners live, or learn from someone from that society. The place of no retribution is heaven. The place where all is forgiven is heaven. All the residents of heaven have been forgiven by God. The person who came from that culture is Jesus Christ. In John 8:23 "…He said … I am not of this world." In John 15:19 He said we are just like Him. "… you are not of the world, but I have chosen you out of the world, …" Paul says "For our citizenship is in heaven, from which also we eagerly wait for a Savior, the Lord Jesus Christ;" (Philippians 3:20).

We know Jesus practiced the culture of where He is from, heaven. Forgiveness is an aspect of the heavenly culture. He invites us to practice it just as He did. Hear His very words on the cross as He died at the hands of those who despised Him: "Father forgive them for they know not what they do."

A culture of forgiveness will be marked by specific elements, namely: Acceptance, Humility, Mercy without Condemnation, Restorative Justice, Tender-heartedness, Dependence on God and Love.

Acceptance

Genesis tells us that God made us in His image and likeness. We are all reflections of God and by creation we are the children or offspring of God. In heaven, everyone is accepted. No one is a stranger or alien. No one left out or seen in a negative or inferior light. There is no diversity committee in heaven, no equal opportunity laws, no affirmative action officer. The heavenly atmosphere is saturated with molecules of acceptance. Jesus demonstrated it at the home of Simon. In Luke 7:36-48, Jesus was invited to dinner at the home of a Pharisee named Simon. He reclined to eat in the way usual to the elite Greeks and Romans. When a prostitute found out that Jesus was eating at Simon the Pharisee's house, she brought an alabaster box of ointment, stood at his feet behind him weeping, and began to wash his feet with her tears, and wiped them with the hairs of her head, and kissed his feet, and anointed them with the ointment.

On seeing this Simon said in his heart, if Jesus was really a prophet, he would have known who and what kind of woman was touching Him. And Jesus answered the thoughts of Simon's heart with a question.

"A certain creditor had two debtors: one owed five hundred pence, and the other fifty. When they could not pay, he forgave them both. Which of them will love him most?" Simon answered "the one he forgave most." Jesus said "you are correct." And he turned to the woman, and said "Simon, do you see this woman? When I entered your house, you did not give me water for my feet: but she is washing my feet with her tears, and wiping them with the hairs of her head. You did not kiss me upon welcoming me to your house: but this woman has not ceased kissing my feet. You did not anoint my head with oil but this woman has anointed my feet with ointment.

Therefore, her sins which are many are forgiven; for she loves much: but those who are forgiven little, love little." Jesus then said to the woman, "Your sins are forgiven." Jesus accepted her despite her checkered past. He let her touch Him and defended her when she was being put down. In a culture of forgiveness, acceptance is a treasured virtue, based upon the belief that all of us belong to a single family and we are integrally connected to each other. Martin Luther King Jr[23]., once said ... "we are all tied together in a single garment of destiny–I can never be what I ought to be until you are allowed to be what you ought to be." Acceptance leads to forgiveness. Jesus forgave the sinful woman of her sins.

---

[23]http://www.democraticunderground.com/discuss/duboard.php?az=view_all&address=132 x3658418

Humility

In Romans 12:3 Paul writes "For I say, through the grace given unto me, to every man that is among you, not to think of himself more highly than he ought to think; but to think soberly, according as God hath dealt to every man the measure of faith." In other words, get rid of all pride and have the spirit of humility or meekness, which is the fruit of the spirit.

Humiliation sometimes produces humility in us. Jesus humbled Himself even to dying on the cross. Roman crucifixion was the most torturous form of execution. Jesus was stripped of His clothing, spit upon and His face was battered until He was not recognizable. He was whipped until His back was lined like plowed furrows ripped into His bare flesh, by bits of bone and metal attached to the ends of the multi-tailed whip used to scourge Him. He was made to carry a heavy wooden cross to a place called Calvary, where He was nailed to that cross.

His tormentors dared Him to come down from the cross, accused Him of being a deceiver, said He saved others but could not save Himself. He heard their taunts and jeers through His pain, His blood and tears.

Innocent of Potiphar's wife's charges, Joseph in the prison was not as humiliated as Christ on the cross.

Job the man of integrity on the dunghill was not as humiliated as Jesus on the cross.

Jesus was the most humiliated and became the humblest person that ever lived. His humility is evidenced in His act of forgiving His executioners, when He could have wiped them off the earth with one word. He chose not to take revenge but to accept the humiliation and forgive. Hear His sincere, loving words from a heart of deepest sorrow and tender humility: "Father forgive them, for they know not what they do."

Mercy without Condemnation

Leah, a beautiful, single, young woman was a first-year Medical Student at an Ivy League Medical School. She was filled with promise and brimming with excitement. When she walked into the church, with her older sister, the members were happy to have them join their little congregation. These young women had moved away from their home in another country and the Pastor and membership adopted them as their own. They were a blessing to the church and the members got very close to them. Leah, like her sister, was busy in the church ministries. She was a Praise Team member, a teacher, prayerful believer and was usually available for a variety of duties.

Everyone loved and admired her and was very proud of her, Medical Student and all. They encouraged her in her education and helped her when and where they could. The church was traditional and the leaders were older and conservative. Leah began dating Troy, a church member, but they were incompatible. Leah was heart-broken when they broke up. No one was aware of how badly she was affected.

One Sunday she went to the Pastor and confessed. "Pastor, I have made a grave error. I am pregnant and the baby's father and I do not even have a relationship." "I used to be like this and I had stopped but with the way things have been going for me I fell back into sin." The look on her face said it all. She was repentant for sinning against God. Her dream of becoming a doctor was now in jeopardy. She was sorry that she had disappointed her Pastor and church family and was worried how everyone at church would feel about her, especially the leaders who were like parents to her.

The Pastor spoke with the leaders and encouraged them to show her Christ-like love. He asked them if they would meet with her and they gladly agreed. As she entered the room and sat down she could almost hear their hearts beating with love for her. "Hold up your head" said one mother, "we are here for you" chimed in another. "We love you, you know." They began hugging and loving on her. She was crying with joy as she felt the love of a forgiving church pouring out on her. The baby was born and the church enjoyed them for several years before they moved away.

The church had a developed culture of forgiveness. Leah was corrected and she submitted to the loving discipline of her forgiving church. The church showed mercy without condemnation, as their goal was to restore her to fellowship.

Restorative Justice

The religious leaders dragged her and threw her down before Jesus. "We caught her in the very act of adultery," they said, "The Law of Moses orders us to stone such persons. What do you say?" They were trying to trap Jesus in His words so they could bring charges against him.

Jesus said nothing but just stooped and wrote with his finger in the dirt. They insisted that He answer, so He said, "if you are sinless throw the first stone," again he bent down and continued writing in the dirt. The accusers began walking away, one after another, from the oldest to the youngest. The woman was left alone and Jesus asked her, "… where are your accusers? Does no one condemn you?" "No one Master," she replied "Neither do I condemn you, go and sin no more." Restorative Justice is an essential element of a culture of forgiveness. Jesus' method of dealing with this adulterous woman was holistic.

Her behavior was sinful, disruptive and destructive to the society. Though she was deserving of condemnation, He did not condemn her. The ones who brought her to Him no longer condemned her, when Jesus gave them the opportunity, to take a fresh look at her sin through the lens of their own sins. Notice, that by exposing the woman's sin to Jesus, the religious leaders had actually been exposing their own sins to all. Jesus corrected them without accusing them. They felt they were the victims of the horrible crime of adultery. Adultery was a gross violation of their society, a rupture in their seamless cloak of self-righteousness.

Jesus asked them to come out from under their cloak and look at the woman again. Jesus forgave the woman's accusers and healing began in their hearts. I would imagine that they would never again be quick to accuse anyone else of anything. The woman was healed and put on a stringent regimen designed to remedy her problem, "Go and sin no more." Finally, the onlookers and the ones who heard what had happened in their city that day were healed as the entire scene unfolded without blood-shed. The accusers were now willing to restore the accused woman to society and Jesus restored her to God, when He said, "Neither do I condemn you." Restorative Justice seeks to help and heal victims, offenders and society as a whole.

Dependence on God

Here is a story of a young man who trusted in and depended on God, to handle the offenses of his assailants that he forgave.

"I started my senior year of college in the fall of 1992 with big plans for a rewarding, lucrative career. My dreams for a great life danced in my head just like the leaves from the trees that lined my street, sauntered in the gentle fall breezes. Life in a Mid Atlantic city is exciting and promising and for me it was a season of hope being fulfilled. Bill Clinton was on his way to the White House, American prosperity was on the horizon, life was just great! News reports of gang activity and random acts of violence resulting in loss of life seemed distant and not relevant to my context.

Then one day, a bullet from the gun of a drive-by shooter penetrated the left side of my face and exited on the opposite side through my neck. Falling to the ground, I went unconscious and began bleeding profusely. Lying in a hospital bed for months and suffering excruciating pain, I clung to life with every labored breath. The only explanation I have for survival and recovery is the mercy of God. The bullet miraculously travelled across my face and neck without affecting my vocal chords.

I later learned that the shooter was an unknown family member. I could not go back to college. The shooter had derailed my life. The very thought of what I had undergone caused me deepest grief. Depression, pain, fear and anxiety dragged me down into a vortex of resentment and anger.

I could not go on living like that, so I surrendered my life to God and placed the matter in His loving hands. I was innocent and I had suffered unfairly. I experienced so much hurt, just like Jesus.

As I grew in the Lord I learned that I could appropriate my experience to identifying with and knowing Jesus, in other words: 'In the fellowship of His suffering.' Yes, the pain was real, the grief was stinging, the inclination to revenge seemed the likely course of action but I chose to forgive. The power of forgiveness destroyed the yoke of bitterness. Bitterness and resentment could have caused me to regret the series of events.

However, the details of the tragedy have become a part of my testimony to young people and to many in prison. God loves them so much that He spared my life and preserved my faculties so I may share the Gospel with them.

I depended on God to heal me of the pain and I trusted Him to change the heart of my offender, with the power of His forgiving love. There are some situations we just need to leave in the hands of God and depend on Him to fix things!"

When you forgive someone, and you ask them to forgive you and they refuse to, what should you do? When people forgive each other, can the relationship between those two people be the same afterwards as it was before? The answer to both these questions is that there are some things you just leave to the Holy Spirit to handle. You really do not rely on, or place your trust in the offender you have chosen to forgive, but you place your trust in and rely on God.

The Lord is well able to resolve and solve anything that impacts our lives. Proverbs 3:5 tells us to "trust in the Lord with all your heart and do not lean on your own understanding."

Some things you will never understand. All God expects you to do is to trust Him!

Tender-hardheartedness

Ephesians 4:32 says "And be ye kind one to another, tenderhearted, forgiving one another, even as God for Christ's sake hath forgiven you." When people do not forgive at times it is because their hearts have become hardened and a hardened heart cannot be easily penetrated. Only God can soften and penetrate a hardened heart.

Tender hearts forgive. Tender hearts leave the offenders in the hands of God. God said in Ezekiel 36:26: "A new heart also will I give you, and a new spirit will I put within you: and I will take away the stony heart out of your flesh, and I will give you a heart of flesh." In a Culture of Forgiveness, tenderheartedness will be the norm. Being compassionate, caring, preferring others and like Jabez, *having no desire to harm anyone*, will be the pleasant fruit of a Culture of Forgiveness.

Love

Love is possibly one of the most discussed, sung about, explained, defined and illustrated topics in all of human history, religion and philosophy. Xochiquetzal, Hathor, Oshun, Yue Lao, Eros and Cupid are named gods and goddesses of love in myth and life in antiquity. In contemporary Western Culture, Saint Valentine's Day, February 14, is set aside to celebrate love. Love has been discussed and celebrated, revered and esteemed throughout human history. Celebrities, poets, singers, musicians, songwriters, novelists, scientists, intellectuals, monarchs, politicians, war generals, housewives and soap operas speak of love. From Wuthering Heights to Romeo and Juliet, from Casablanca to the Hunchback of Notre Dame, love reigns in regal splendor. Popular art about love, like "The Kiss"[24], provokes and stimulates the love dialog. Songs such as Wonderful World, I Say a Little Prayer, Let's Stay Together, My Girl and At Last, are considered immortals of the pop charts. Beyonce, American singer, songwriter and actress is not silent on the subject of love. From Love Drought to Drunk in love and Dangerously in love, Beyonce's songs say she is love struck or love stuck.

Notwithstanding; mythology, art, literature, history, religion, and even music all fall short of being able to adequately express love to the human soul. In addition, around the idea of love there is so much confusion, misinformation, aggravation, perversion, anxiety, trouble and pain. Humanity seems to be on an elusive search for the mysterious treasure called love. Our ancestors fought this battle and their progeny are still in mortal combat in the pursuit of true love.

---

[24] http://www.huffingtonpost.com/2012/09/05/the-kiss-a-celebration-of_n_1854535.html

Like a mirage, it disappears before the eyes of humankind and leaves Adam's fallen race weary, thirsty, hungering, empty and defeated. It seems like the human quest from time immemorial is where or what is love? Is it real? The answer is yes! And real love is sacrificial. It displays a willingness to freely give its all for the benefit of another as Gerald did for Dee.

Nothing seemed unusual as Gerald and his 16-year-old daughter Dee, drove south-bound on the motorway. Cars and trucks whizzed passed them on their left and right. Out of nowhere, a truck from the northbound lanes hurtled out of control, crossed the median and landed on the roadway in front of Gerald and Dee. With no time to think, Gerald swerved his car to avoid a head-on collision.

When emergency crews arrived, Dee was safe though she had suffered a few scratches and scrapes. Her dad, Gerald, was crushed to death upon impact. Dee remembered her dad swerving the car, to prevent her side from crashing into the truck. By doing so, he took the full impact on his side, upon collision. Gerald gave his life for Dee.

Gerald's love for Dee is like the love God demonstrated in Christ for us all. "In that while we were yet sinners, Christ died for us." Christ practiced love and He has invited us to love one another. A culture of forgiveness is characterized by love.

I have met and read of people who died or had near death experiences and were restored to life. A good book on the subject is titled <u>Heaven is for Real</u>. In another book, titled <u>Proof of Heaven</u> by Neurosurgeon, Eben Alexander, the author's near death experience took him to heaven.

The colors he saw in heaven are unlike anything he had ever seen. He describes the very atmosphere of heaven as being so clean and serene. He describes the activities and actions of those residing there and he concludes that the operations of heaven take place through the medium of love.

Love is the lubricant, engine and operating system of heaven. Heaven's very character, nature and culture harks of love. The entire environment is saturated with the presence of God. God supports and supplies heaven with everything it needs and it is obvious that it will be drenched with love because "God is love."

A culture of forgiveness will only function with and by the power of love. Love will soothe the heart of the offended. Love will bring the offender to her/his knees. When love walks in the door, hate jumps out the window. Love banishes revenge, retribution and retaliation. Love restores, reconciles, heals and remedies, until we are made whole to perpetuate a Culture of Forgiveness, a culture in which we forgive one another from the heart.

Pray this prayer:

"Dear Lord I pray for our world. I pray because unforgiveness forms the very fabric of our social relations. This culture is destructive and unproductive. We have become so accustomed to revenge, hate, retaliation and retribution that it seems normal to strike back. O Lord change me. Change me O Lord until I become forgiving like Jesus. Let this change be experienced by everyone who has confessed Christ. Remove the cobwebs of un-forgiveness. Clothe Your Church in the garment of forgiveness until our forgiving lifestyle influences our world for Your glory. In Jesus name. Amen!"

Chapter 7 Review

1. List and discuss the indicators of a culture of forgiveness.
2. When you tell someone you forgive them and they become angry and refuse your forgiveness what should you do?
3. Explain Restorative Justice.
4. Discuss and describe Gerald's love for Dee.
5. Love is the operating system of heaven. Discuss.

Chapter 8

CŞ

From the Heart

"God is able to forgive you and give you the grace to forgive those who have wounded you."

Matthew 18:35 "So My heavenly Father also will do to you if each of you, from his heart, does not forgive his brother his trespasses."

"The dark screen on my iPhone stared up at me as it lay silently on the floor. All I needed to do was to pick it up, hit the home button, retrieve the contact number and call him. This call was three years overdue and I still did not want to make it. 'Get over it, suck it up, let bygones be bygones leave it to God is the prevailing wisdom. All of that is easy to say but much harder to do. I thought that I had done it all but still felt a knot in my stomach and the often headaches, when I remember how I was treated and who I thought was responsible. My pain was real and regardless of whether I was right or wrong I had not gone the distance to forgive from my heart.

Whether you admit it or not, when you feel or think that someone smiled in your face and stabbed you in the back repeatedly, you would not want to call them. Their words are like daggers that you know would pierce your soul but call I must and I did.

This was the first step on my way back to the spiritual and emotional health I so desperately needed. I waited as his phone rang a few times for about five seconds but it seemed much longer. Then he answered. There was a time when he knew my voice but his hesitation in responding when I said "hello," hinted to me that he was not sure. I identified myself and his response was cordial. It sounded like he was almost pleased to hear from me after so long. The months of agony were painful and relentless. From anger to frustration, from questioning to complaining, I had spent the last thirty-six months hurting deeply for the loss of a friendship that had lasted almost two decades. But now we were on the phone and after a brief greeting I simply said, 'I am calling to tell you that I forgive you. What happened between us has hurt me deeply but I just want to put it behind me, I am not going to carry this with me for the rest of my life, so I forgive you.'

In that moment, it seemed that a dam broke and a torrent of pent up emotion made its exit from my mind. I was free now and whether he took it as I meant it or he became angry with me for trying to come over as 'super-spiritual' or as 'holier than thou' it was over for me. I felt free. To my great surprise, he too was ready to put this behind us. He expressed his regrets for how things turned out with us and he said, 'I apologize.'

We reminisced a bit about our work together in years gone by, he wished me well and encouraged me to stay in touch. I turned off the phone and felt so relieved because I had forgiven. I had forgiven him from my heart. Forgiveness from the heart is genuine forgiveness.[25]"

---

[25] *Experience of Dr. Wayne C. Solomon*

Countless people are trapped in a web of unforgiveness. Their minds reel in confusion, their emotions are frayed and daily they function below their optimal levels because in their hearts, they carry the dead weight of the ones they have not forgiven.

It is very clear to me from scripture that true forgiveness comes from the heart. The word heart here refers to the thoughts and feelings or the mind. This term comes from a Greek word transliterated *kardia* that by analogy means the middle[26]. The heart therefore is the middle or the center of our being.

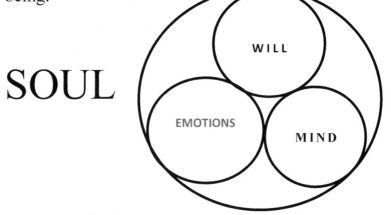

The human is a three part being that is a spirit who lives in a body and has a soul. Between the human body and the human spirit lies the soul,

---

[26] The Expanded Vines Expository Dictionary of New Testament Words

which is the center or the middle of the human. Hebrews 4:12 delineates the parts of the human: "For the word of God is quick, and powerful, and sharper than any two-edged sword, piercing even to the dividing asunder of <u>soul</u> and <u>spirit</u>, and of the <u>joints and marrow</u>, and is a discerner of the thoughts and intents of the **heart**. When Adam and Eve sinned in Eden, which part of their beings originated the sin? Spirit? Soul? Body?

First, let's look at the human spirit. Humankind was made with an eternal human spirit. Hence it was perfect. Humans lived in fellowship with God so their spirits were protected by God. The devil could not get to the humans' spirits. Next, their bodies were eternal human bodies. Since their bodies were the medium of their expressions on the earth and their contact with the natural realm, their bodies were open to the influences from the natural realm. But their bodies were not responsible, for without the spirit and soul the body cannot function. And besides, the Edenic environment was perfect.

The earth was not corrupt and nature was pure. The spirit and the body were not responsible for originating humankind's sin. Therefore, it is obvious that it was the soul that was responsible.

The soul is made up of the emotions, the mind and the will. We can only do wrong or right because God has given us the ability to choose, by virtue of having given us free will. So, since the will is in the soul, the soul of humankind, described as the heart in our text, is the place where sin originated and still originates today.

"But those things which proceed out of the mouth come forth from **the heart**; and they defile the man." (Matthew 15:18)

"For out of **the heart** proceed evil thoughts, murders, adulteries, fornications, thefts, false witness, blasphemies: these are the things which defile a man:" (Matthew 15:19,20).

We contemplate the life of righteousness in our hearts.

"But the righteousness which is of faith speaketh on this wise, Say not in **thine heart**, Who shall ascend into heaven?" (Romans 10:6).

We believe with our hearts, to be saved.

"And Philip said, If thou believest with all **thine heart**, thou mayest." (Acts 8:37).

"That if thou shalt confess with thy mouth the Lord Jesus, and shalt believe in **thine heart** that God hath raised him from the dead, thou shalt be saved. For with the heart man believeth unto righteousness; and with the mouth confession is made unto salvation." (Romans 10:9-10)

We pray from our hearts

"Flee also youthful lusts: but follow righteousness, faith, charity, peace, with them that call on the Lord out of **a pure heart**." (2 Timothy 2:22).

Therefore, genuine forgiveness should come from the heart. "So likewise shall my heavenly Father do also unto you, if ye from **your hearts** forgive not everyone his brother their trespasses." (Matthew 18:35).

Since sins arise in the heart, when we are offended our hearts are affected. In our emotions, anger arises, from our minds pride emerges. Our intellects rationalize and reason that we should not forgive, because we are in the right. Our wills become bent on revenge. These tendencies of the heart need to be curbed for genuine forgiveness to take place. We must forgive from the heart if we are to truly effect remission or true release of the offender.

When we speak about the origin of the word heart or *Cardia,* it is the same word we use in medicine today. It is where we get the word 'Cardiac' it means heart related. The heart is one of the hubs or centers, in terms of organs of the body. It is the main pump. Without a heart the brain will not function.

The function of the heart is to pump blood throughout the body, including the brain. If your heart is not working, the chances are you will die, unless we substitute the heart. Either we give you a heart transplant or today we have "artificial hearts," but though their function is the same, they are not the same as the real human heart. I want you to grasp that the heart is the center. That's the reason why someone can say 'I forgive you,' with the lips, but if it did not originate from the heart, it is useless!

If a poison or an infection enters a vein from any part of your body it goes throughout the body because the heart is pumping it. It is pushing it; it is spreading it throughout the whole body, because the heart is at the center or hub of the circulatory system.

Un-forgiveness spreads like an infection or poison throughout your life. It affects you psychologically, physiologically, spiritually, relationally, economically etc. Sooner or later it is going to be exported and pumped out to others. Un-forgiveness is contagious! Un-forgiveness breeds and cedes more un-forgiveness, which is why our world is an unforgiving world. So Jesus focused on forgiving from the very inner core, the very center of our being, the heart.

As discussed in chapter 1, Matthew 18 records a parable that describes the kingdom of heaven as a king that took account of his servants. One servant owed him a large sum of money and was unable to pay. So, the king commanded that his family and he and all he had be sold in order to make payment. The man begged for patience, promising he would repay. The size of the debt was so much that there was no way he could repay it. But because the king had compassion, he forgave him his debt. (Ancient Oriental kings were often extreme. Sometimes they were extremely cruel or extremely kind. They were not always predictable and acted on impulse).

The forgiven servant left the king's presence free from debt. On his way home, he met someone that owed him a small sum of money. He demanded his money and when the debtor asked him to have patience, promising that he would repay, the forgiven servant would not show mercy but instead, he had him arrested and thrown into prison demanding that the debt be paid. When his fellow servants saw what had taken place, they related it to the king. The king told the forgiven servant, 'I forgave you all that debt because you asked me for mercy, and should you not have had compassion on your fellow servant even as I had pity on you?'

When we came to the Lord, He forgave us from all our sins. Every human being is born in sin and shaped in iniquity. Sinful humanity is powerless and cannot escape the weight, burden and consequences of sin. We are in great debt to God, but the moment we say 'God have mercy on me,' God forgives us of all our sins. In light of this, it does not seem unreasonable for God to expect us to forgive the offences of others against us. Christians are expected to forgive other Christians as well as those who are not Christian believers.

Paul said in Romans 12:18-21 "If it is possible, as much as depends on you, live peaceably with all men. Beloved, do not avenge yourselves, but rather give place to wrath; for it is written, 'Vengeance is Mine, I will repay, says the Lord.' Therefore, if your enemy is hungry, feed him; if he is thirsty, give him a drink; For in so doing you will heap coals of fire on his head. Do not be overcome by evil, but overcome evil with good." (NKJV)

Notice here Paul advises us to take these steps in dealing with enemies:

Avenge not yourselves. Let God take revenge. Revenge is a condition of the heart. When forgiveness springs from the heart revenge will not follow.

If your enemy is hungry, feed him, if he is thirsty, give him to drink. For in so doing you shall heap coals of fire on his head. Let us look at the term, 'heap coals of fire on his head.' Here Oriental customs come into focus[27]. The ancients kept fires in their homes in a clay pot. Coals were kept burning continually in the pot. If this charcoal fire

---

[27] Insights into Bible Time sand Customs by G. Christian Weiss

ever went out, usually a female family member would take the clay pot to a neighbor's house to borrow some live coals. In those countries, back then, almost everything was carried on the head. So, the fresh coals in the clay pot would be lifted on to the head of the one borrowing the burning coals, and she would head home. If the neighbor who gave the coals was a generous woman, she would heap the pot high with fresh hot coals. But if she was stingy she may only give a few tiny embers. Thus, the expression 'heaping coals of fire' is a symbol of the finest generosity and sincerity.

Now, to be kind to a person so as to punish them is also taking revenge. Be careful not to fall into that trap. When you forgive an offender and you begin to be kind to them, it is not to make them miserable, but to make them happy, and soon they too will come to know the Lord, who loved them through you. Heaping coals of fire does not mean taking vengeance using fake kindness. Paul says, 'Vengeance belongs to God.' Do not take revenge.

Martin Luther King Jr., was told that his house had been bombed. When he got home he saw that the porch had been destroyed but his family was unharmed. They were in another part of the house when the bombing took place. Several concerned but angry people, who had rushed to the scene, wanted King to give them permission to retaliate as they knew the bombers. King said "we must love our enemies; we must make our white brothers know that we love them[28]." King believed that "Forgiveness is not an occasional act, it is a constant attitude.[29]"

Further, in Matthew 5:38-45 (NKJV), Jesus said: "You have heard that it was said, 'An eye for an eye and a tooth for a tooth.' But I tell you not to resist an evil person. But whoever slaps you on your right cheek, turn the other to him also. If anyone wants to sue you and take away your tunic, let him have your cloak also. And whoever compels you to go one mile, go with him two. Give to him who asks you, and from him who wants to borrow from you do not turn away. Love Your Enemies.

You have heard that it was said, 'You shall love your neighbor and hate your enemy.' But I say to you, love your enemies, bless those who curse you, do good to those who hate you, and pray for those who spitefully use you and persecute you, that you may be sons of your Father in heaven; for He

---

[28] Strength to Love Martin Luther King Jr., Fortress Press, 1977
[29] https://www.goodreads.com/author/quotes/23924._Martin Luther King Jr.

makes His sun rise on the evil and on the good, and sends rain on the just and on the unjust."

It is clear from this text that we are expected to give special attention to enemies. Jesus' list of requirements for dealing with offending enemies includes:

1. Turning the other cheek if you are hit on the right cheek. Matthew 5:39
2. Giving up your cloak if your coat is wrongfully taken from you. Matthew 5:40
3. Going two miles when asked to go one Matthew 5:41
4. Giving to those who ask of you. Matthew 5:42
5. Lending to those who wish to borrow from you. Matthew 5:42
6. Loving your enemies Matthew 5:44
7. Bless those that curse you. Matthew 5:44
8. Doing good to them that hate you. Matthew 5:44
9. Praying for them that despitefully use you. Matthew 5:44

Now, notice verse 45 of Matthew 5 is connected to the previous verses by the word THAT. "that you may be sons of your Father in heaven; for He makes

His sun rise on the evil and on the good, and sends rain on the just and on the unjust." This infers if you do these things you will be recognized as a child of your heavenly Father. For you would be acting as He does; treating the righteous and the unjust equally and doing good to even those who offended you. God's love is not partial or discriminatory but inclusive, universal, sacrificial and unconditional. He forgives you from His heart of love, and expects you to forgive everyone who offends you from your heart.

Stanley and Liz met at college and got married. Their love was so pure and sincere, that it filled the hearts of the church members with wonder, to see how closely they guarded their relationship. Soon their first child was born and a few years later a second showed up.

Marriage does come with challenges and the business of living in a changing world where values seem to alter so quickly shaking faith, examining beliefs and questioning established principles. Stanley was very friendly and calls from women even visits and casual contacts with them sparked arguments and anger in the home. Liz began to insist that contacts with the women end. He would not be pushed by her and they became distant. Later she began getting the attention of a man at the church. At first, she ignored him but the prospect was appealing and frankly she was flattered by his advances. It was not long before they were stealing away for romantic rendezvouses. Stanley found out and became furious. He thought of ending the marriage. She decided to leave the family and their storybook marriage fell apart, when God intervened. They cried out to Him for mercy, confessed their faults to one another and forgave each other. The Holy Spirit healed their hearts and they began the slow trek back to spiritual, relational and familial health. Over the next several years they healed and have truly forgiven each other from their hearts.

Whatever the source of your offense, God is able to forgive you and give you the grace to forgive those who have wounded you.

Pray this prayer aloud:

"Lord I have longed for a closer relationship with you. I have sought You in prayer, meditation, fasting and worship. I have no desire for the things that are fleeting, things that do not satisfy or fill the void in the human heart. I want to be more like You. I want my heart to be like Yours. I want to feel deep compassion in my heart for all who have offended me. I need the grace to forgive those who have wronged me from my heart. I do not want to carry the pain of un-forgiveness any more. I do not want my life to be stuck in the alleyways of revenge, retaliation and retribution. I do not want to be consumed with fears of rejection and anticipations of bad outcomes. I do not want to be wrapped in the garments of anger and rage, frustration and depression. Heal my hurting heart. Heal it until it gets whole, so I can forgive those who hurt me from my heart, in Jesus name. Amen!"

Chapter 8 Review

1. Define the human being according to the author. Discuss the Bible verse in Hebrews that shows the distinction of the parts of the human.
2. Explain *kardia*.
3. Discuss the makeup of the human soul.
4. The soul and the body are connected via the emotions and the nervous system. Discuss.
5. Who said "we must make our white brothers and sisters know that we love them"? Discuss his philosophy of love.

Chapter 9

❧

Lethal Weapon

"Never fight the devil on his turf, fight him on ours. Our turf or our part of the battlefield is a minefield of love, joy, peace, faithfulness, long-suffering, kindness, meekness, temperance, self-control and our Lethal Weapon, Forgiveness."

Luke 23:33-34 "And when they were come to the place, which is called Calvary, there they crucified Him, and the malefactors, one on the right hand, and the other on the left. Then said Jesus, 'Father, forgive them; for they know not what they do."

Movie great, Clint Eastwood, is known for his famous words: "Go ahead, make my day." Arnold Schwarzenegger's tough guy words are:

"Hasta la vista, Baby" and Mel Gibson's penchant for violence earned him a salacious designation. His detective partner, played by Danny Glover, labeled him when he said, "I guess we will have to register you as a Lethal Weapon." In the movie, so named, Gibson leaves a trail of dead bodies, blown up cars and buildings in his wake. He is hailed a hero, a guardian of the innocent, a protector of the weak because he destroys his enemies with the force of a Lethal Weapon.

There are numerous powerful weapons invented by humans. Russia detonated the most lethal weapon in history during the Fall of 1961, the Tsar Bomba, a Hydrogen bomb which was 1570 times the power of the bombs that destroyed Hiroshima and Nagasaki. It destroyed property as far as 170 miles around, its mushroom cloud was 40 miles high, and it sent shock waves as far as 430 miles away. But more lethal than super-bombs and super-heroes in destroying enemies, is the Lethal Weapon of Forgiveness.

Prior to his rise to fame in his 1860 Presidential Election, Abraham Lincoln's, noteworthy adversary was Pittsburg Lawyer, Edwin Stanton. Upon being inaugurated President in 1861,

Lincoln selected Stanton to be his Secretary of War. Startled by this choice, his friends and critics quizzed Lincoln about what seemed an unwise political decision. Lincoln questioned in response: "Do I not destroy my enemies when I make them my friends?"

Though the word frenemy has gained momentum, partly because of the contemporary contradictions we live with, friend and enemy categories are mutually exclusive. If you are a friend you cannot be an enemy and if you are an enemy, you cannot truly be a friend. No one can be faking it and making it at the same time. So, friendship annihilates enmity. Enmity ends when the offended forgives the offender. Forgiveness is lethal to enmity.

Here is a story in the life of Noreen who deployed the lethal weapon of forgiveness. "She never imagined the day would come when her life would be hanging by a thin thread. Doctors and nurses were working feverishly to keep her alive. Even if she lived, what quality of life would she have? She would be no more than a vegetable, dependent on people, medication and machines to keep her dying body alive.

The darkness covered her eyes. She had not seen light since the orange and blue flashes from the nozzle of the gun lit the dark room. Silence had since enveloped her, after she heard the cracking blast, from the hand gun aimed at her from point blank range. Her attackers kidnapped her, took her to an undisclosed location where she was assaulted. Then the shots rang out into the night, two rounds at least, were fired directly into her head. The brutal assailants fled the scene leaving her to bleed to death.

Miraculously she was found, rushed to a hospital and a competent, experienced team of emergency room doctors prepared her for surgery. Neurosurgeons employed their skills with laser like precision, to remove the bullets and repair the damage done to the head and brain. Other doctors were tending to her bodily injuries sustained from the assault as well as the effects of blunt force trauma, sustained in various parts of her body. Somebody wanted Noreen dead and it looked like they were getting their wish.

The medical team did not see much hope for recovery, but they pressed on, using the latest technology available and with the help of some of the most brilliant minds, they managed to remove all but two of the bullets lodged in her head. She was unconscious for weeks, in a coma; it was just a matter of time before they would pull the plug and take her body to the morgue.

Then, amazingly she opened her eyes and progress began its march, until Noreen was Noreen again. When you see her shopping in the mall, caring for children, functioning efficiently at her job and singing at church, you would never know that she still has two bullets in her head. Noreen had been through a grueling ordeal and she knew who had done it to her. Her psychological pain increased as she thought of the ones who were free to walk around and continue their brutal lifestyle while she languished in the pain of her experiences.

Revenge seemed a delicious dainty that tempted her daily. Wishing that her assailants would die in a car crash or shooting, her mind was trapped by the pain. 'O God why did you let this happen to me? Why did You not just let me die in the hospital? Why did I have to suffer like this and they go free? It is so hard to forgive, so hard to let go, so hard to move on with my life.' In her depression and heart-breaking grief, Noreen cried out to God to soothe her heart and destroy her desire for revenge. God healed her and soon she began to forgive her attackers and release them from her heart. With the Lethal Weapon of forgiveness, Noreen had destroyed enmity and un-forgiveness. Like Jesus, Noreen had reason and the means to retaliate but she did not. She was innocent but she chose to forgive."

The most powerful detonation of the Lethal Weapon called forgiveness took place when Jesus was on the cross. Luke 23:33-34 records this event as follows: "And when they were come to the place, which is called Calvary, there they crucified Him, and the malefactors, one on the right hand, and the other on the left. Then said Jesus, 'Father, forgive them; for they know not what they do.'" With those words, Jesus destroyed the power of the sin of un-forgiveness. He refused to engage in retribution but determined to pour out His life's last drop of blood, with the soul-cleansing power of forgiveness. THIS ACT OF JESUS WAS THE MOST POWERFUL WEAPON EVER DEPLOYED! IT DESTROYED ALL SIN AND THE POWER OF SIN. Forgiveness was provided for all who come to God in repentance and in faith.

Forgiveness from the heart, when deployed annihilates psychological and emotional pain. Healing takes place when someone forgives, as it releases them from hate, revenge, retaliation, retribution, grudges, rancor, fear, suspicion, gossiping, backbiting, dislike, disloyalty, rage, anger, distrust and mistrust. Forgiveness eliminates plots for murder and acts of betrayal. Forgiveness prevents the misdirected anger that manifests in domestic violence and child abuse. Forgiveness lowers the risk of heart diseases, ulcers, headaches, indigestion, acid-reflux, dementia, Alzheimer's, diabetes, depression, gastrointestinal problems, and asthma. Forgiveness restores us to functioning at our optimal levels. This means that we can become more productive.

Un-forgiveness can hurt us economically. Just think about the number of people that work who are suffering from un-forgiveness. They cannot give their all and their best at work. Their work is impaired and the business place loses revenue. Conservatively speaking, if 25% (or 40 Million workers[30]) of the US workforce is operating at 75%

---

[30] http://www.dlt.ri.gov/lmi/laus/us/usadj.htm

of their optimal level because of un-forgiveness: using the US Median income ($55,750.00[31]), the loss to the US economy in one year will be $557,750,000,000.00 (five hundred and fifty-seven billion, seven hundred and fifty million dollars). If the Lethal Weapon of forgiveness is deployed, the economy can be boosted.

Individuals, steeped in un-forgiveness, can do themselves untold financial harm because of underperformance at work, as this may result in termination. My advice is to deploy the Lethal Weapon of Forgiveness. Forgiveness will destroy financial ruin, sibling rivalry, arguments, separation, divorce, anger, fights, disrespect and unkindness in families.

Finally, note this, we are in battle against an enemy who wants to destroy us. Ephesians 6 tells us that we are not fighting against flesh and blood entities but demonic beings marshalled by satanic powers. These forces try to lure us onto their territory of the battlefield. If we fight them on their part of the battlefield they will have an advantage over us.

---

[31] http://www.deptofnumbers.com/income/us/ (2015)

Un-forgiveness, hate, revenge, retaliation etc. make up their territory. When we fight like satanic and demonic forces fight we are on their turf. What we need to do is to bring them onto our turf and have home court advantage. Never fight the devil on his turf, fight him on ours. Our turf or our part of the battlefield is a minefield of love, joy, peace, faithfulness, long-suffering, kindness, meekness, temperance, self-control and our Lethal Weapon, Forgiveness. Fight like this and you will ultimately win!

Pray this prayer and deploy the Lethal Weapon of Forgiveness:

O Lord I come again to You who made the heavens and the earth. In Your perfect mercy, You poured out your loving compassion upon my soul. It seems that troubles have come from every side and I can no longer hide. Much of my pain is directly linked to offenses I have suffered. People have lied on me, cheated me out of what is mine, hurt my family and tried hard to cut me off from the few friendships I have left. They have spoken evil of me and betrayed me so many times that I have lost count. Their faces are before me day and night and I cannot get them off my mind. My stomach becomes knotted when I remember what they have done to me. I just wanted to live a quiet life, showing kindness to all and giving of myself to those I could help. But they have taken advantage of me and robbed me of my peace of mind. These things have affected me physically, as my body has suffered pain. My head would begin to ache, my chest would hurt, and my breathing would sometimes be difficult. I have been a bit dizzy at times but I just keep on going. This thing has hurt me emotionally. I have felt the pangs of fear, the fierceness of anger, the stranglehold of worry and the turbulent torrents of anxiety. Lord I am aware that these matters will be resolved when I forgive those who offended me, so help me to blast these troubles away with the Lethal Weapon of Forgiveness. I forgive those who lied on me. I forgive those who stole from me. I forgive those who speak evil of me. I forgive those who I thought were my friends and they betrayed me. I forgive them, I release them, I unload the heavy weight of un-forgiveness and I free my soul to rise to new heights in God. Be free my soul, climb up to Zion's lofty heights. Be free my soul, escape the prison cells of un-forgiveness, break the iron bars of retaliation, smash the brass gates of retribution, push down the stone walls of revenge, smash the locks of hate, snap the chains of slavery and be free my soul, be free to live again, to love again, to laugh again, to praise again, to worship again, Be free again my soul, in Jesus name. Amen!"

Chapter 9 Review

1. Discuss how Abraham Lincoln used the Lethal Weapon of forgiveness.
2. Forgiveness destroys psychological, physical and economic troubles. Explain.
3. Write a lethal weapon prayer to give to someone who has been hurt.

Chapter 10

CB

Heart Transplant

"For a heart to be made available for transplant, the donor must die. The Donor, our Donor, Jesus Christ died. He died to give us a new heart."

Ezekiel 36:26
"I will give you a new heart and put a new spirit within you; I will take the heart of stone out of your flesh and give you a heart of flesh."

"When you can move from Florida to Alaska to co-parent with someone who hurt you deeply, you know you have forgiven them from the heart!"
The winds of Midwestern America that sweep through the plains and city streets of that flat region relentlessly, often gain tornado status leaving

property damage, injury and loss of life. Leaving doors open is never an option, especially in the spring and fall months of the year. Tree limbs snap and fall to the ground, traffic signals swing dangerously above as motorists speed hastily under them.

In the winter months, the wind chill is a meteorological reality mid-westerners all too well understand. Twenty degrees Fahrenheit could easily feel like nine degrees below zero. Thick coats and sturdy boots, scarves and earmuffs that hold down ski-masks, wool-lined gloves and woolen socks are standard gear to face snowy winter mornings. Whenever you need to walk across an icy parking-lot to enter a building, caution takes precedence over speed.

As Pastor Josey Thompson drove into the lot at the Doctor's Office for his annual checkup, his main concern was getting from the car to the doorway of Suite 1743, without slipping on the treated but quite icy walkway. Dr. Goldstein had been his doctor for more than seven years. He always had great reports following his checkups. Dr. Goldstein had Josey's lab-reports, EKG, Echocardiogram and stress test results, and was ready to discuss them, when Josey climbed unto the doctor's examination table. "How are you feeling Josey?" Dr. Goldstein asked. "Quite well, except for shortness of breath every now and then." Dr. Goldstein then stated, "Your test results indicate that your heart is not working right." "What exactly is wrong doctor? What are you saying?" asked Josey anxiously. "Josey, based on the results of your tests, it appears that your heart is very weak and is not pumping blood to the rest of your body adequately. This means you will need a heart-transplant." "Your heart is deteriorating rapidly and at this stage it is inoperable." Josey's heart sank.

He began to think about his wife, Sandy, their two small children and his congregation. For the next two years, his life was touch and go. Josey was on the donor list for a heart transplant. He lived in constant expectation of getting the news that a heart had become available. Then he would have to drop everything he was doing and head to the hospital for preparation to receive the transplant. Josey's breathing was difficult, worst with activities and at bedtime when he laid down to sleep. He could not walk very far without resting for a while. He was not allowed to lift anything above ten pounds. His condition deteriorated day by day and anxiety for a heart increased. If it did not come soon he would be restricted to bed rest and eventually die, or placed on an artificial heart machine, which he refused.

Then one day, the special cell phone he was given for the transplant, rang. "Hello, is this Mr. Thompson?" "Yes" replied Josey. "Doctor Goldstein would like you to report to the cardiac unit right away for your transplant." "I will be there in thirty minutes." "That will be just fine." With that, Josey picked up his keys and his wife drove them to the Hospital. The procedure took place the next morning. It lasted for six hours and it went well.

The heart was compatible and Josey was placed in the cardiovascular Intensive Care Unit. He was expected to be there for a few days because no complications were anticipated. Josey woke up to see his wife's smiling face. Doctors, nurses and technicians had been in and out, monitoring Josey's vital signs and observing his recovery, at ten to fifteen minutes intervals. Josey's pain was being managed by medication and he was in good spirits.

Two days later, Josey asked Doctor Goldstein if he knew whose heart he was given. "Well, Josey I do not know and even if I did, that information is classified. No one, including me, would be at liberty to disclose it. You understand, don't you Josey? The transplant recipient counsellors, no doubt explained the challenges that could arise for the program if that information gets out. Some limited information can be obtained after you recover."

Six weeks after he was discharged Josey was even more curious. He went to the hospital to track down the information. He found out that his new heart had come through Organ Transplants Network. Josey got their phone number and called their office with his question. "Mr. Thompson, the agreement concerning the identity of donors is designed to protect both the recipient and the donor's family members. This information is strictly confidential, said the pleasant voice on the other end. "I understand, but I just must know. Can you make an exception?" pleaded Josey. "Maybe you can come to our offices and speak with the director."

The following day Josey drove over to the quiet neighborhood on the west side of town. The staff was very hospitable and friendly. A well-dressed woman in her forties came to the waiting area and invited him to her office. "Mr. Thompson, I am so happy you could come in. I am Laura Russell, Director of Organ Transplants Network." "Thank you for seeing me" said Josey. He began, "I know that my request is not unusual and you follow strict policies and guidelines, but I just need to know. I am a Pastor and I want to thank the family members of the donor. I want to let them know that their loved one's heart saved my life and that I will live a good life, to honor their loved one's memory."

Laura had heard many requests, but somehow she was moved by Josey's sincerity. "I rarely make this information known to recipients and donors' family members. However, in your case I will make an exception." She continued, "Can you give me your phone number? I will see what I can do." Laura took the number and walked with Josey back to the waiting area. Later that same day Josey got a call. "Is this Josey Thompson?" asked a man that sounded like he was in his fifties. "Yes sir" Josey said. "I heard you wanted to know about the heart you got" said Marcus. "Yes, I do sir" answered Josey nervously. Marcus asked, "Can you come to our home tomorrow?"

Josey obtained the address and arrived around six the next evening. The house was at the end of the street in a cul-de-sac. Rose and Marcus Long were at the door to greet Josey and his wife, Sandy. They seemed awed as Josey approached them. The four went to the parlor and sat down. For a good three minutes, no one spoke, then Rose broke the ice, "Marcus and I have been married for twenty-three years. Erin turned twenty-two last October" as she handed Josey a picture of the young, beautiful Erin, dressed in a baby-blue gown with a white-rose corsage on her right wrist.

"You have her heart. I am so glad to see you" Rose said smiling. Erin's Dad, Marcus, picked up the conversation, "I have tried and tried to stop grieving but it seems like it won't go away," he explained, then continued: "She was so young and healthy. She played soccer and ran track you know. I cannot believe she is gone. When you walked in I felt as if she was here." A full minute of silence ensued, then Josey began, "Mr. and Mrs. Long, I cannot tell you how grateful I am. I promise you, and I promise God I will honor Erin's memory, by serving God and our world to the best of my ability. Her heart is keeping me alive."

"I know her heart keeps you alive but you are keeping her heart living" said Marcus Long. "And because you have her heart, to me it is as if she is still alive. Thank you for coming Josey and Sandy. Thank you Josey for what you promised. We will always remember this meeting." Josey and Sandy drove home. Neither spoke much for the entire fifty-seven minutes it took to get back to their neighborhood.

There were none of the usual winds, just a gentle breeze that blew the colorful flags at the corner store. Rounding the corner at the entrance of their street, Josey breathed a prayer for Marcus and Rose as he remembered the face of the young, beautiful Erin who died so he could live.

God spoke through the prophet Ezekiel and said: "I will give you a new heart and put a new spirit within you; I will take the heart of stone out of your flesh and give you a heart of flesh." Coronary disease is the number one cause of death worldwide. Hearts fail to function when they are deprived of air that contains life giving oxygen. When a person experiences a heart attack, CPR or cardiopulmonary resuscitation, delivers air to the heart and revives the patient. Some heart conditions cannot be remedied and the patient needs a transplant. Such is the condition of humanity. The prophet Isaiah declared "...the whole heart *is* faint."

Ezekiel describes the condition of the human heart as a heart of stone. That heart, Ezekiel declares, God will replace with a heart of flesh. Jesus came to give the human race a new heart. For a heart to be made available for transplant, the donor must die. The Donor, our Donor, Jesus Christ died. He died to give us a new heart. He died to take our hardened, diseased, dying heart and gave us His tender, healthy, whole, loving, living, forgiving heart.

This new heart is transplanted into our lives by the Holy Spirit. When we accept this new heart; the heart, *cardia*, the very center of our being emits, disburses and pumps life throughout our entire being. This new heart, emanating life, perfumes our relationships, restores our spiritual strength, heals our emotional wounds and reconnects every part of our being. Our new heart is supplied, refreshed and sustained by the life-giving wind of the Holy Spirit.

To maintain a spiritually healthy heart, a heart like Jesus' that forgives, the believer must allow the Holy Spirit to imbue her/his life with the nutrients: love, joy, peace, longsuffering (patience), gentleness (kindness), goodness, faith (faithfulness), meekness and temperance(self-control). A life-long pursuit of the child of God is to be filled with the Holy Spirit. In the case of a heart-transplant recipient, it takes time for the new heart to function normally in the recipient's body. Nothing may be wrong with the heart itself, but the recipient's body must adjust to the new heart and synchronize its systems, to the functioning and rhythm of the new heart.

So too the Christian's new heart, obtained from Jesus, will require the other aspects of the believer's life to come into harmony with its rhythm. The recipient of a new heart must change his/her diet to maintain a healthy heart and therefore a healthy life. The Christian must change his/her spiritual diet to maintain a strong spiritual life and a loving, giving, forgiving heart. The spiritual nutrients necessary for this new lifestyle includes, worship, prayer, fasting, the Word of God, fellowship and service. Like Pastor Josey Thompson in our story, the recipient of a transplanted heart should be relentless in her/his search to know about the person who gave the heart.

A lifetime search to know more and more about Jesus will continue to resupply the believer with the impetus to nurture a loving, giving and forgiving heart. When a person has such a heart, that heart will keep them alive spiritually and they will keep the Christ-like life alive, for all to see when they forgive from the heart.

Pray this prayer:

"Dear God, my heart has been hardened because I have been offended. My pain is so great and I feel like I will never be normal again. I don't like having a hard heart. I don't enjoy feeling angry all the time. This whole thing has affected my relationships and it seems like I filter many of my actions, words and thoughts through the lens of the offense. I cannot do this anymore. It is not working for me. I have prayed before but now I pray specifically again. Lord I need a spiritual heart transplant. Take my heart of stone and give me a heart of flesh. Take my hateful heart and give me a loving heart. Take my heart of retaliation and give me a heart of reconciliation. I want to be restored to my offender. I want to turn off the faucet of bitterness and open the streams of Your healing love, until I can forgive everybody everything, in Jesus name. Amen!"

Chapter 10 Review

1. What spiritual parallels are there to be drawn from heart transplants according to the prophet Ezekiel?
2. Explain how we keep Jesus' heart alive in us.
3. Discuss the work of the Holy Spirit in forgiveness.
4. Write a prayer (of at least 50 words) of submission to God for a spiritual heart transplant.

Epilogue

The three days ended and I was heading back to Florida. Philip and I experienced spiritual bliss as we spent time in God's presence. Fasting has a way of releasing great spiritual boosters into our lives. During a good fast, the flesh is subdued and the spirit rises, the mind is renewed and the will yields to God. Our hearts were made so much more sensitive to the urging of the Holy Spirit to forgive anyone who had wronged us. I had made one call to extend forgiveness. I am on the road to restoration of my relationship with my friend! It still feels a bit awkward, but I understand that the rest of my being, is still adjusting to my transplanted forgiving heart. I have others I need to contact as God gives me the grace. I really do not feel the degree of hurt I had felt prior to my going to New Jersey. I am healed. Like some who have served in ministry, I have been used and abused, betrayed and taken advantage off. I have been lied on and misunderstood, set-up and maligned, robbed and taken for granted. The pain has been deep and destructive, intense and severe. I have experienced depression, anxiety, worry and anguish of all kinds, but the healing breath of the Holy Spirit, has regenerated my heart and filled me with a humble desire and resilient determination, to forgive everybody for everything. It is not perfected, but my forgiving heart is pumping its healing life throughout my being, and day by day I find it easier to forgive from the heart. I don't know what tomorrow will bring, but I simply place it all in His holy hands and choose to live my life, loving and forgiving not hating and retaliating.

Philip drove me to the airport and I boarded the economy airline flight from Trenton to Orlando. Later that day he called me. "I made the call" he said. "You did?" I asked. "Yes, I did. I had to do it. I cannot be teaching about forgiveness and not practice it myself," he replied. I admire Dr. Philip Bonaparte for his honesty and humility. He continued "I called him and said 'I forgive you.'" I could hear the earnestness in Philip's voice. Earlier in his ministry, Philip served at another church and there were some challenges that he endured. He said to me some time ago, "It was difficult for me, but I submitted myself to spiritual authority and served as best as I could. When my wife and I planted the church thirteen years ago, I faced opposition. The attacks and offenses hurt me. I don't want to nurse those wounds anymore. I decided to make the call and I did."

Philip has turned the whole matter over to God and he is now free from the heavy weight that was upon him. In our last Facebook Live Bible Study on Forgiveness, Dr. Bonaparte explained: "When you fail to forgive someone, it is like they are tied to you and you carry them everywhere you go. They hold you back and retard your progress, restrict you and limit your ability to function at your optimal level. The only sensible thing to do is to release the person who offended you, so you can live your life without hindrance." In Matthew 18:35, Jesus said that God will forgive us when we forgive others from the heart.

Endorsements

Dr. Philip Bonaparte and Dr. Wayne Solomon have collaborated to write and provide an excellent resource to the Body of Christ. *Forgiveness From The Heart* is indeed true forgiveness. Anything else, falls short of the ultimate freedom that comes, when one truly walks in the graceful spirit of remission and pardon. Both of these Christian leaders are long-time students of the Word of God, successful Pastors and helpful leaders of humankind. You will learn, be encouraged and equipped for ministry as you read this excellent book.

Dr. Timothy Hill
Presiding Bishop Church of God
Cleveland, Tennessee

This Book is a subject that is so necessary for discussion. I'm very glad my friend and brother, Wayne Solomon, has taken the time to pour this helpful book into our lives! We should never forget forgiveness is a gift, that we must give ourselves. So many of us say daily we want to be like Christ. Well, we are more like Christ when we practice forgiveness. You see, when we forgive, we give up our right to hurt others who hurt us. When all we see is our pain, we lose sight of God. Therefore, forgiveness is the key to our inner healing. So, the real question is: Can God trust you with trouble? Remember, He's using your trouble to prove a point to others about His love.

Bishop Brandon B. Porter
Greater Community Temple COGIC
General Board Member Church of God In Christ

A culture saturated with unforgiveness and vengeance will never thrive or experience true "shalom." Only a radical transformation of the heart can guarantee change and relational healing. In this most comprehensive book, the authors provide an incisive examination of the debilitative effects of unforgiveness and the biblical path to wholeness and restoration. Indeed, this is a "must read" for enjoying total freedom.

Bridgelal Seenath, D.Min.

162

You hold in your hand an invitation to learn about the transforming power of forgiveness and loving-kindness. In this wise and well-written book, Wayne Solomon and Philip Bonaparte have gathered a treasury of insights from time-honored Biblical principles for bringing healing, peace, and compassion into our daily lives, so that we can face intentional or unintentional offensive behaviors of others that can cause disillusionment and bitterness, because of something that was said or done. The authors' brilliant insight into forgiveness shines through on every page, and they are clearly teaching the reader that forgiveness is a process and that it is painful to hate others. When we forgive, the heart can be released from the most painful circumstances. Solomon and Bonaparte's book is a "go-to" resource for anyone involved in weighted-down toxic thoughts and emotions of un-forgiveness and is a valuable resource for every hurting heart.

Bishop Hugh Bair, D.Min, Ph.D.
Christian Life Church – Baltimore, Maryland

In Forgiveness From The Heart, Bonaparte and Solomon reveal the anatomy of this Christian virtue that is so vital to our world. This volume will stir your soul and challenge you to Forgive from the heart. I recommend this book wholeheartedly.

Clifton Clarke PhD
Associate Dean, Fuller Theological Seminary

Forgiveness From The Heart is an energizing journey unearthing God's healing plan for the disease of un-forgiveness. Philip Bonaparte and Wayne Solomon's insights and Scriptural exegesis uncover transformational truths to overcome the spiritual stagnation of un-forgiveness. The moving accounts of numerous persons who have forgiven their offenders will resonate with all who are in the throes of conflict, and lead them to inner peace through Forgiveness From The Heart.

Dr. J. David Stephens
Second Assistant General Overseer
Church of God, Cleveland, Tennessee

"My dad, Andrew, who is 87, received a booklet by Dr. Wayne Solomon on *Forgiveness* 30 years ago and he still preaches from it today. That book has helped him see many lives transformed including his own. This new book, <u>Forgiveness From The Heart,</u> is even more informative and inspirational. I am deeply moved by this insightful volume. It reminds me that forgiveness is THE HEART of all things. Forgiveness is the cross. Forgiveness is love. Forgiveness is God. Excellent book!"

Andrew and Lennox Rattansingh, BSc MBA
CEO of National Maintenance Training and Security Company Ltd
Trinidad and Tobago

God desires that we live life at the speed of favor however, the enemy uses un-forgiveness as a weapon against the bible believer. In the book "<u>Forgiveness From The Heart</u>", Dr. Wayne .C. Solomon and Dr. Philip M. Bonaparte Sr. expose spiritual offenses, free emotional hurt and deliver from hindrances that block the blessings of God. This must read book shares practical biblical principles and spiritual insights from years of experience that brings healing, restoration, freedom and deliverance. As you read this treasured book, it reveals the heart and love of Jesus Christ while defining a culture of forgiveness. Each chapter is relevant to the time we are living in and offers the believer power to subdue the spirit of un-forgiveness. "True forgiveness is treating the person the way you treated them prior to the incident." My prayer is that your life will be transformed by God, who will give you a new heart, new revelations and new levels of favor.

Dr. Tony Barhoo
Founder and Senior Pastor
Living Faith World Ministries
Daytona Beach, Florida
Area Director of World Harvest Church Ministerial Fellowship
Columbus, Ohio

About the Authors

Wayne Solomon was born again at the early age of eleven. He is the husband of Monica Squires Solomon and the father of Candace and Crystal Solomon. Dr. Solomon is an Ordained Bishop in the Church of God and Adjunct Professor of Sociology and Religion at Lee University and the Pentecostal Theological Seminary (PTS). He has served as Administrative Bishop of the Church of God Florida Cocoa and of the Great Lakes Region. He is founder of Maranatha Tabernacle in Rhode Island where he served for 22 years and the New Testament Church of God Claxton Bay Trinidad where he served for 9 years. He has been involved in the planting and organizing of over 100 churches in the United States, Trinidad and Tobago, Guyana and Ghana West and in the training of over 1200 ministers. For 18 years he was the Director of Ministerial Development in Southern New England. He holds a Doctor of Ministries Degree in Leadership, Master's & Bachelor's Degrees in Sociology and Associate Degrees in Human Services, Theology and Business Management. He obtained his education at PTS, Brown University, Harvard University, Rhode Island College, Quinnebaug Valley Community College, the University of the West Indies, and the New Testament Church of God Bible Institute of Trinidad and Tobago. Bishop Solomon is the author of books such as: *When the Fire Falls, Closet Religion, Keep it and Lose it or Lose it and Keep it, Pray Christian Pray, Endoonamoo, Unshakeable Faith in God, Sword of the Spirit, Brokenness to Blessings, Guard Your Anointing, I Feel Like my Hair is Growing Back, Get up and Try,* as well as co-author of *Ministering to Culturally Diverse Populations.*

Philip M. Bonaparte, M.D is married to Tracey S. Bonaparte and is the father of Philip II and Philicia. Rev. Bonaparte gave his heart to the Lord at the age of 15 and began preaching the gospel of Jesus Christ at 19. He founded the Woodlands New Testament Church of God in Grenada and now serves as Lead Pastor of New Hope Church of God in New Jersey, one church in three locations: East Windsor/Hightstown, Trenton and Long Branch. Bishop Bonaparte is District Bishop and member of the Church of God NJ State Ministers' Council. He is also a member of the Church of God Cleveland, TN International Care Ministry Board. His unique ministry, Medical Doctor and Minister has afforded him opportunities to address a variety of audiences. He is host of two national radio broadcasts that he uses to preach the Gospel. Dr. Bonaparte leads a daily 6:00am Prayer Line –(Your Spiritual Workout) that attracts over 500 callers. He is founder and Chief Medical Officer of the New Hope Health Center, providing Free Health Care, for the uninsured and underinsured residents of NJ. As a Medical Doctor of 28 years he is Board certified in Internal Medicine and is currently licensed to practice in NJ. He was Chief Medical Officer of Horizon NJ Health for over 11 years and an officer of Horizon Blue Cross and Blue Shield of NJ for five years until his retirement in 2013. Prior to Horizon, Dr. Bonaparte was Senior Vice President of Medical Affairs for Robert Wood Johnson University Hospital at Hamilton and remained an attending physician on staff for over ten years. He played an integral part in the screening, prophylaxis and treatment of individuals in the 2001 Anthrax Exposure at the post office in Hamilton, NJ. He is recipient of many awards: the State of NJ Governor's Council on Mental Health Stigma 2016 Ambassador Award, UIH Family Partners 2016 Platinum Dad Award, 2015 & 2016 NJ State District Overseer of the Year, 2014 NJ Pastor of the Year, 2014 Positive Community Choice Award for Health, 2011 Humanitarian Award from the American Red Cross Northern New Jersey Chapter and the 2011 Leadership Award from the Caribbean Medical Mission.

Forgiveness from the Heart

Made in the USA
Columbia, SC
23 February 2025